Silver Burdett Ginn Science

DiscoveryWorks

SCIENCE NOTEBOOK

ACTIVITIES

UNIT PROJECTS

INVESTIGATE FURTHER

CREDITS
Contributing artist
Sarah Jane English

ISBN 0-382-33513-9

7 8 9 10 H 05 04 03 02 01 00

CONTENTS

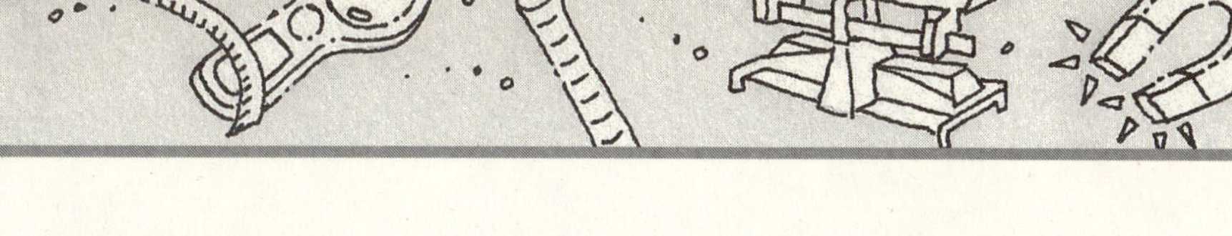

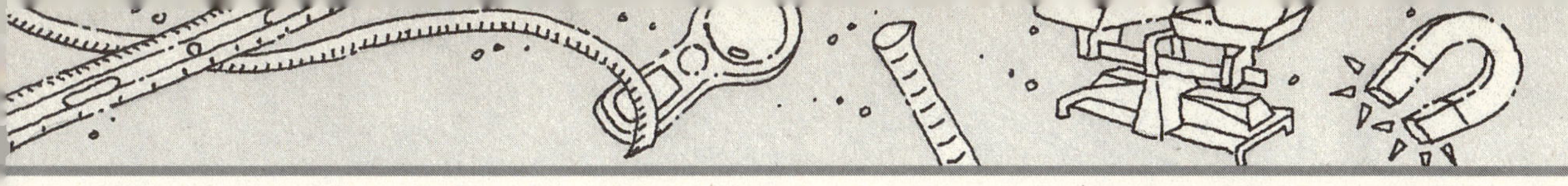

UNIT F   FORCES AND MOTION 311

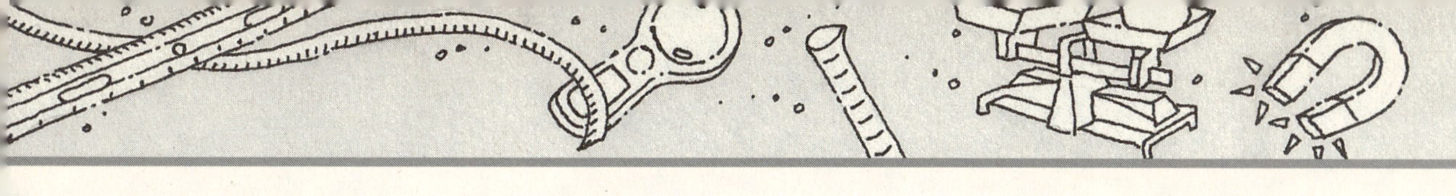

UNIT
A

Name___________________________ Date__________

CELLS AND MICROBES

In Unit A you'll learn about the cells of living things and about microscopic organisms. In the Unit Project Big Event, you'll build models to exhibit in the Great American Microscopic Zoo. What is a cell and what does one look like?

____

____

____

____

____

What are the different kinds of microscopic organisms and what do they look like?

____

____

____

____

____

What kinds of cells and microbes would you want to include in a microscopic zoo? Explain why.

____

____

____

____

____

Name____ Date____________

UNIT PREVIEW

Consider what you know about cells and microscopic organisms.
What are some additional things you'd like to learn? On the lines
below, list your ideas.

Name ________________________________ Date ____________

CELLS

Draw what you think a cell from an animal and a cell from a plant look like. Be sure to draw what you think is inside the cells.

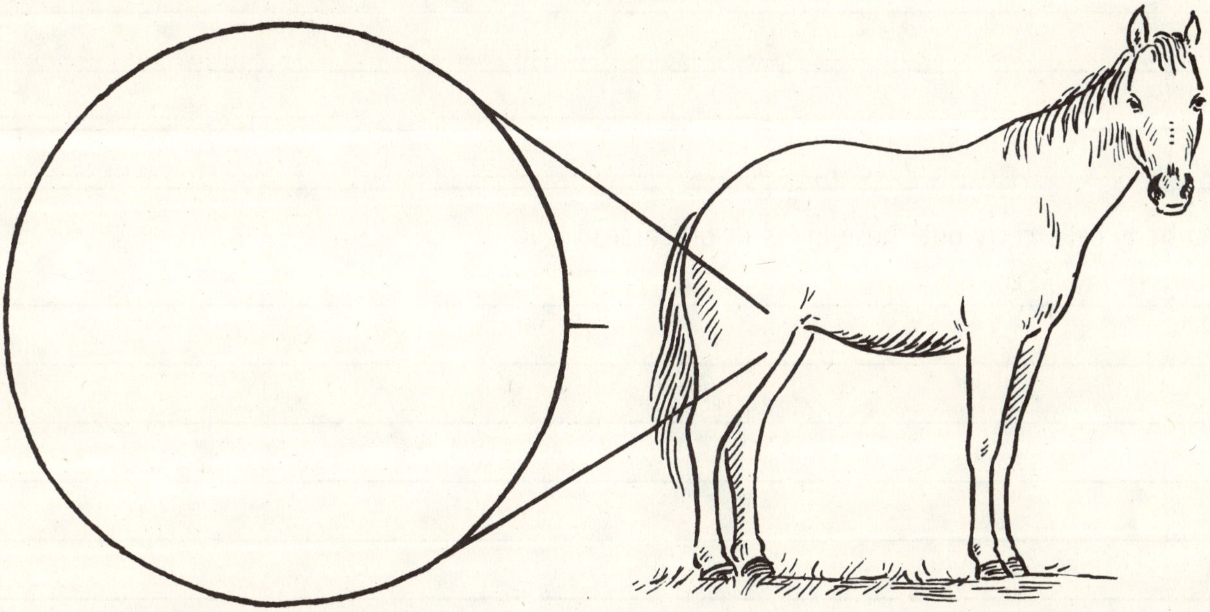

Name _______________________ Date _______

Dear Journal,

All cells in my body have these features in common . . .

____

____

____

____

____

____

My body cells carry out these kinds of processes . . .

____

____

____

____

____

____

A process that plant cells can perform but animal cells cannot is . . .

____

____

____

____

I think the way that cells make more cells is . . .

____

____

____

____

____

Name ________________________________ Date __________

OBSERVING PLANT CELLS

Procedure

Make a drawing of what you see when you observe the slide of a small piece of the *Elodea* leaf under low power.

Make a drawing of one *Elodea* cell that you can see when observing the slide under high power.

Label the cell wall and the chloroplasts in your drawing of the *Elodea* cell.

Label a vacuole and the cytoplasm in your drawing of the *Elodea* cell.

Write a description of differences you observe in the *Elodea* cell when you repeat steps 2 through 4 using the salt solution instead of aquarium water.

____

____

____

Make a drawing of the onion cell under high power. Label the nucleus and other structures you see.

ACTIVITY RECORD

Name _________________________________ Date _________

Analyze and Conclude

1. ____

____

2. ____

____

____

Draw what you observe of the tomato skin under high power.

Compare what you see in the tomato cell with what you saw in the onion cell.

Infer the reason for the differences you observed.

ACTIVITY RECORD

Name _________________________________ Date _________

OBSERVING ANIMAL CELLS

Procedure

Record your observations of what you see when you observe the cheek cells under low power.

____

____

Make a drawing of one cheek cell as seen under high power.

Record your observations of what you see when you observe the slide of frog blood under low power.

____

____

Make a drawing of one frog blood cell as seen under high power.

Analyze and Conclude

Write the answers to the questions in your book on the lines below.

1. ____

____

____

Name _______________________________________ Date ___________

2. ____

____

____

3. ____

____

____

____

Record your observations of the differences between human red blood cells and frog blood cells.

Infer why this difference exists.

Record the sources you used in your research.

UNIT PROJECT LINK

Name____ Date__________

UNIT PROJECT LINK

Identify a specific kind of plant or animal cell that you would like
to build a model of. Give reasons for your choice.

____

____

____

____

____

How can you find out what shape this cell has and what specific
structures it contains?

____

____

____

____

What materials could you use to build a model of this cell?

____

____

____

____

How large should the model of this cell be compared with the models of other types of cells?

____

____

____

Share this information with your group.

Name ____ Date ___________

INVESTIGATION 1

1. You are observing two unlabeled cells. What can you look for to determine which is a plant cell and which is an animal cell?

____

____

____

2. Why do scientists infer from the cell theory that all living things are related?

____

____

____

____

Make a chart that summarizes what you have learned about the parts of cells. Indicate the names of the various parts, whether they can be found in plants or animals or both, and what their function is in the cell.

Name _________________________________ Date __________

MOVING IN AND OUT OF CELLS

Procedure

Write your prediction of what will happen when you place the bag containing the starch mixture in contact with the iodine solution.

____

____

____

Make a chart in the space below on which you can record your observations of the setup every 15 minutes for 2 hours.

Analyze and Conclude

Write the answers to the questions in your book on the lines below.

1. ____

____

2. ____

____

____

Name _______________________________________ Date __________

3. ____

____

____

4. ____

____

____

INVESTIGATE FURTHER!

EXPERIMENT

Page A15

Predict how you will be able to tell if diffusion takes place when you repeat the activity using food coloring instead of iodine.

Record your observations of what happens when you repeat the activity using food coloring in the beaker instead of iodine.

Infer from your observations what occurred in your setup over the 2 hours.

Name _______________________________________ Date __________

INVESTIGATION 2

1. How is diffusion important to cell processes such as photosynthesis?

____

____

____

____

____

2. How might your life be affected if your cells contained chloroplasts?

____

____

____

____

Make a diagram that shows a cycle formed by oxygen and carbon dioxide in which plants and animals take part.

Name _________________________________ Date _________

MULTIPLYING BY DIVIDING

Procedure

Record your observations of where you located cells on the root tip that look like the photographs on page A21.

____

____

____

Draw a diagram to record what you think the sequence of photographs should be.

Analyze and Conclude

Write the answers to the questions in your book on the lines below.

1. ______________________________________

____

____

2. ______________________________________

____

3. ______________________________________

____

Name _________________________________ Date _________

INVESTIGATE
FURTHER!
....
RESEARCH

Page A21

Record what you learned about cloning.

What cell material do scientists work with when cloning in the
laboratory and where in the cell is that material located?

Record the name of the sources you used for your research.

Name _______________________________ Date __________

INVESTIGATION 3

1. When a cell divides, how do the two new cells end up with the correct number of chromosomes?

____

____

____

____

____

2. Why do the cells in multi-celled organisms specialize?

____

____

____

____

____

Make a flow chart that shows how cell differentiation results in an organ system.

CHAPTER WRAP-UP

Name ____ Date ____________

CELLS

What are the main points of the cell theory?

____

____

____

____

____

Name the parts of a cell. What parts do plants cells have that animal cells don't have?

____

____

____

____

____

What are some life processes of cells? Describe three.

____

____

____

____

____

How do cells make more cells? Describe mitosis.

____

____

____

____

____

CHAPTER WRAP-UP

Name _________________________________ Date _________

Think about what you learned in Chapter 1 when you answer the following questions.

1. How do you think about your own body now that you have read "Cells"?

____

____

____

____

____

2. What did you learn in reading the chapter that changed your understanding of something you thought you knew?

____

____

____

____

____

3. What was the most difficult concept for you to understand as you read the chapter? What could you do to understand it better?

____

____

____

____

____

Name _________________________________ Date _________

PROTISTS AND FUNGI

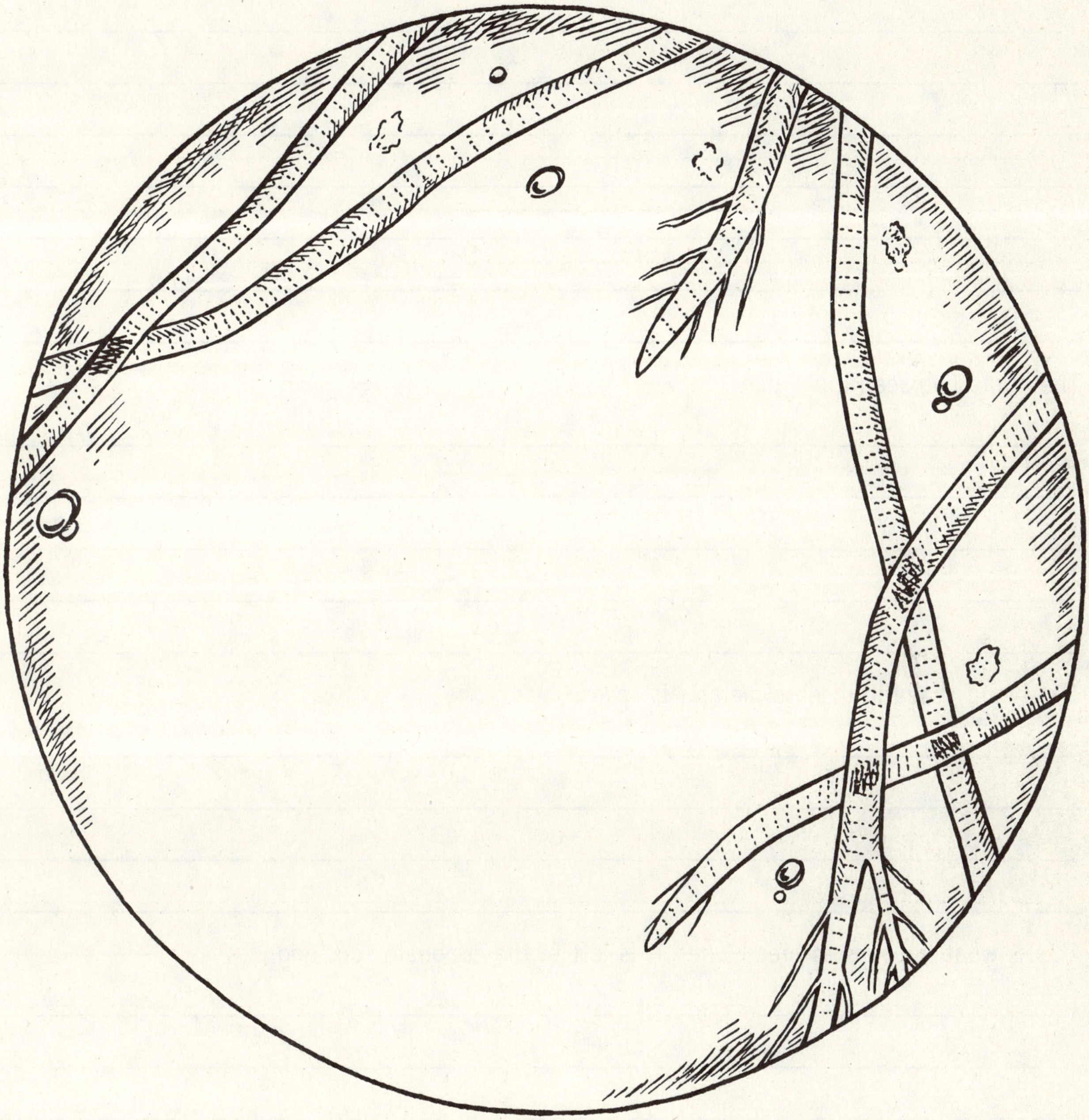

What do tiny single-celled organisms look like? What structures do they
have to get themselves around? Draw some organisms you might see if
you looked at pond water under a microscope.

Name _______________________________ Date _______

Dear Journal,

My understanding of what single-celled organisms are like is . . .

____

____

____

____

____

____

The algae I've seen looks like . . .

____

____

____

____

____

I've heard that the disease malaria is spread by . . .

____

____

____

____

This is what happens to bread when it is left in the cupboard too long . . .

____

____

____

ACTIVITY RECORD

Name ___________________________________ Date __________

MICROORGANISMS

. . . .

Procedure

Make sketches of any tiny organisms you see when you examine the drop of pond water under the low power and the high power of the microscope.

Analyze and Conclude

Write the answers to the questions in your book on the lines below.

1. ____

____

____

2. ____

____

____

3. ____

____

____

Name ___________________________________ Date ___________

OBSERVING AN ANIMAL-LIKE PROTIST

Procedure

Make a drawing of an amoeba that you observe
on the slide under low power.

Make drawings of the same amoeba two or more
times, at 1-minute intervals.

1 minute later:

1 more minute later:

1 more minute later:

Name _______________________________________ Date _____________

Write a comparison of the amoeba on your slide with the one in the photograph on page A31.

____

____

____

____

____

Analyze and Conclude

Write the answers to the questions in your book on the lines below.

1. ____

____

____

____

2. ____

____

____

____

Name _________________________________ Date __________

OBSERVING A PLANTLIKE PROTIST

Procedure

Write your prediction of how a plantlike protist may be different from an animal-like protist.

____

____

____

____

Record your observations of the *Spirogyra* specimen on the slide with the microscope at low power.

____

____

____

Make a drawing in the space below of several *Spirogyra* cells.

Analyze and Conclude

Write the answers to the questions in your book on the lines below.

1. ____

____

____

ACTIVITY RECORD

Name _______________________ Date __________

2. _______________________________

____

____

____

3. _______________________________

____

____

Describe the cause of sleeping sickness and how people become infected with the disease.

Record where in the world the disease is most common and how it might be prevented.

Describe the cause of amoebic dysentery and how people become infected with the disease.

Record where in the world the disease is most common and how it might be prevented.

Name _________________________________ Date __________

INVESTIGATION 1

1. A friend of yours insists that all protists are microscopic. Write a letter to that friend, explaining why this statement is not true.

____

____

____

____

____

2. Choose one of the protozoans you studied and imagine you are that organism. Write one day's entry in an imaginary journal of that protozoan.

____

____

____

____

____

Euglena is a single-celled organism that is both plantlike and animal-like. It's shaped somewhat like a paramecium, but without the cilia. It has a flagellum to get around. It also has a nucleus and a light-sensitive eyespot. Like a plant, *Euglena* contains green chloroplasts. From this information, make a drawing of what you think *Euglena* looks like.

Name _______________________________________ Date _______________

LIFESTYES OF FUNGI

Procedure

Write your prediction of what the best conditions are for growing mold.

____

____

____

Make a drawing of what you see with the hand lens when you observe
the slices of bread through the plastic bags after they have been left for
several days.

Make a drawing of the small piece of mold you observe under the microscope at low power.

Name ____ Date _____________

Make a drawing of the small piece of mold you observe under the microscope at high power.

Write a description of the conditions under which mold grows best once you have compared your results with those of your classmates.

____

____

____

Analyze and Conclude

Write the answers to the questions in your book on the lines below.

1. ____

____

____

2. ____

____

____

____

UNIT A

UNIT PROJECT LINK

Name_______________________________________ Date__________

UNIT PROJECT LINK

Identify a specific fungus or protist that you would like to build a
model of. Give reasons for your choice.

____

____

____

____

How can you find out what structures this organism has so that
you can accurately build the model?

____

____

____

____

What materials could you use to build a model of this organism?

____

____

____

____

How large should the model of this organism be compared with the
models of other cells and organisms?

____

____

____

____

Share this information with your group.

Name _______________________________________ Date ___________

INVESTIGATION 2

1. How can fungi and plants be distinguished?

____

____

____

____

____

2. Why do fungi not require light in order to survive?

____

____

____

____

Draw a humorous cartoon that shows how a saprophyte cleans up the environment.

Name _________________________________ Date _________

PROTISTS AND FUNGI

What are protists?

____

____

____

____

Describe how an amoeba captures its food.

____

____

____

____

What is plankton and what protist makes up a large part of it?

____

____

____

____

What are the different types of fungi and how do most get their food?

____

____

____

____

Name _________________________________ Date _________

Think about what you learned in Chapter 2 when you answer the following questions.

1. What was the most interesting thing you learned as you read "Protists and Fungi"?

____

____

____

____

____

____

2. What did you see through the microscope that you will never forget? Explain why.

____

____

____

____

____

____

3. What did you study in the chapter that you would like to learn more about? How could you find more about that subject?

____

____

____

____

____

____

Name _________________________________ Date __________

BACTERIA AND VIRUSES

Draw a picture that shows how you think the common cold can be spread from person to person in a classroom.

Name _____________________________ Date __________

Dear Journal,

Bacteria and viruses are similar and different in these ways . . .

____

____

____

____

____

____

Some diseases caused by bacteria and viruses are . . .

____

____

____

____

____

____

I think ways to fight diseases caused by bacteria and viruses include . . .

____

____

____

____

____

The way that the disease AIDS affects the body is . . .

____

____

____

____

Name _______________________________________ Date _____________

CLASSIFYING BACTERIA

Procedure

Record your observations of the different kinds of bacteria shown in the photographs on pages A48 and A49.

____

____

____

____

____

____

Make a classification of the kinds of bacteria shown in the photographs. Classify them into groups, and give reasons for your classification.

____

____

____

____

____

Analyze and Conclude

Write the answers to the questions in your book on the lines below.

1. ____

____

2. ____

____

Name____ Date____________

UNIT PROJECT LINK

Record the results of your research on one of the types of bacteria.

____

____

____

____

____

____

Write the names of the sources you used in your research.

____

____

____

From your research, what materials would you want to use in building a model of this type of bacteria?

____

____

____

____

How large should the model of this type of bacteria be compared
with the models of other cells and organisms?

____

____

____

Share this information with your group.

Name _______________________________________ Date ___________

INVESTIGATION 1

1. A person looks at a cell through a microscope and thinks it's a plant cell. You look and see that it's a bacterial cell. Explain to the other person the features of the cell that allow you to draw your conclusion.

____

____

____

____

2. Describe how viruses affect living cells.

____

____

____

____

Draw a pyramid-shaped diagram that illustrates how scientists classify the different kinds of monerans.

Name _______________________________ Date _________

WARM MILK

Procedure

Write your predictions of what will happen to the milk in the bottle kept in the refrigerator and the milk in the bottle kept at room temperature.

____

____

____

____

Record your observations of the differences between the milk in the two bottles after letting the bottles sit for two days.

____

____

____

Record your observations of the smell from each bottle.

____

____

____

Analyze and Conclude

Write the answers to the questions in your book on the lines below.

1. ____

____

____

2. ____

____

3. ____

____

INVESTIGATE FURTHER

Name ______________________________ Date __________

Record the changes you observed after chilling the mixture in the refrigerator for at least 12 hours.

Infer how the bacteria you added to the milk caused the changes you observed.

Compare the yogurt you made with a commercial yogurt you can buy at the store.

Make a flow chart that describes how bacteria are used in the production of one type of food.

Record the names of the sources you used in your research.

Name ____ Date ____________

INVESTIGATION 2

1. How does a person's body fight bacterial and viral attacks? What type of medicine can treat bacterial infections if the body's immune system is not successful?

____

____

____

____

2. Give two examples of ways in which bacteria are helpful.

____

____

____

____

Suppose that you're a doctor and a mother comes to you with her 3-year-old son, Michael, who is ill. You discover that he has swollen glands in his throat, pain when chewing and swallowing, and a fever. The mother tells you that recently Michael's friend had similar symptoms. Use the tables on pages A58–A59 to find a possible diagnosis. Then fill in the medical record below.

Medical Record

Name:

Age:

Symptoms:

Possible diagnosis:

Type of disease-causing organism:

Reason for diagnosis:

Possible outcome if not treated:

CHAPTER WRAP-UP

Name _______________________________ Date __________

BACTERIA AND VIRUSES

What are bacteria and where do they occur?

____

____

____

____

What are viruses and why do they seem to fall between the living and
the nonliving world?

____

____

____

____

How do bacteria and viruses affect other living things?

____

____

____

Describe the relationship some bacteria have with grazing animals, such
as cows.

____

____

____

____

Name _______________________________ Date _____________

Think about what you learned in Chapter 3 when you answer the following questions.

1. What surprised you most as you read "Bacteria and Viruses"? Explain why.

____

____

____

____

____

____

2. What did you read in the chapter that most changed your understanding of the environment around you?

____

____

____

____

____

____

3. What did you learn about diseases that you hadn't known before reading the chapter?

____

____

____

____

____

____

UNIT WRAP-UP

Name_______________________________ Date________

UNIT PROJECT WRAP-UP

Think about the models of cells, protists, fungi, and bacteria that you and others made for the Unit Project Big Event, the Great American Microscopic Zoo. Which model did you like the best? Explain why.

____

____

____

____

How did visitors react to this Micromenagerie? Were they surprised at the variety of organisms shown?

____

____

____

____

____

How did this Unit Project help you learn more about cells and microorganisms?

____

____

____

____

____

If you were to help create a similar display again, what would you do that was different?

____

____

____

____

UNIT PREVIEW

Name_______________________________ Date__________

THE CHANGING EARTH

In Unit B you'll learn about Earth's crust, the building of mountains, and the causes and consequences of earthquakes. In the Unit Project Big Event, you'll help develop a guide on how to prepare for earthquake and volcanic activity. Have you ever experienced an earthquake? If not, what do you think it would be like?

____

____

____

____

What do you think being near a volcanic eruption would be like?

____

____

____

____

What do you think a person should do if he or she suddenly feels an earthquake?

____

____

____

Suppose that you lived in an area that had frequent earthquakes. What safety precautions could you take around the home that might save your life or prevent extensive damage?

____

____

What safety precautions could you take if you lived near an active volcano?

____

____

UNIT PREVIEW

Name_________________________________ Date___________

UNIT PREVIEW

Consider what you know about Earth's crust. What else would you like to learn? List your ideas on the lines below.

Name _________________________________ Date __________

CRACKED CRUST

You're in a submarine near the ocean floor in the middle of the Atlantic Ocean. What "land" formations can you see around you? Draw what you think the ocean floor looks like.

Name _________________________________ Date _____________

Dear Journal,

Earth's crust is composed of these materials . . .

____

____

____

A continent is . . .

____

____

____

We know that the continents have not always been in the same place as they are now because . . .

____

____

____

____

I believe that volcanoes can be found . . .

____

____

____

Scientists make maps of the ocean floor by . . .

____

____

____

My understanding of Earth's magnetic properties is . . .

____

____

____

Name _______________________________________ Date ____________

THE GREAT PUZZLE

Procedure

Make a map on which you fit all of the continents together into one supercontinent. Keep this map in your *Science Notebook*.

Analyze and Conclude

Write the answers to the questions in your book on the lines below.

1. ____

____

2. ____

____

____

3. ____

____

4. ____

____

____

____

Name _______________________________ Date _________

Describe a land formation that seems to match between North America and Europe.

Describe a land formation that seems to match between South America and Africa.

Explain why you think Alfred Wegener hypothesized that Earth's landmasses were once joined as a supercontinent.

Name _______________________________________ Date ___________

INVESTIGATION 1

1. Evidence of glaciers has been found in many parts of southern Africa! What does this information tell you about the possible location of this continent at some time in the past?

____

____

____

____

2. Describe the kinds of evidence that Alfred Wegener and other scientists have used to show that the continents move over time.

____

____

____

____

____

Make a sketch in the space below of the world's continents as they appear today. Then indicate on your map where fossils of *Glossopteris* have been found.

Name _________________________________ Date _________

EARTH—ALWAYS ROCKIN' AND ROLLIN'!

Procedure

Write a description of any pattern or patterns you see in the dots on the earthquake map.

____

____

____

____

____

On tracing paper, trace and then darken the pattern formed by the earthquake dots. Attach this tracing in the space below.

Record your answer to the question about how the pattern of dots is like the cracks of an eggshell.

____

____

____

ACTIVITY RECORD

CHAPTER 1

Name _______________________________________ Date _______________

Analyze and Conclude

Write the answers to the questions in your book on the lines below.

1. ____
____
____
____
____
____

2. ____
____
____
____
____
____

Name_________________________________ Date__________

UNIT PROJECT LINK

How close is your town to the edge of a tectonic plate?

____

____

Predict how likely your town is to have an earthquake.

____

____

____

In the space below, record the data you collect from news articles about earthquakes and volcanic activity around the world.

Share this information with your group.

Name _______________________________ Date __________

VOLCANOES AND EARTH'S PLATES

Procedure

Make a list of the places where volcanoes occur.

____

____

____

____

____

____

____

____

____

Record your hypothesis about the locations of volcanoes, earthquakes,
and the edges of Earth's tectonic plates.

____

____

____

____

Analyze and Conclude

Write the answers to the questions in your book on the lines below.

1. ____

____

____

2. ____

____

____

Name _________________________________ Date __________

INVESTIGATION 2

1. Predict what might happen in 10 million years to Los Angeles (on the Pacific Plate) and San Francisco (on the North American Plate) if the two plates carrying these cities continue to move in the directions in which they are now moving.

____

____

____

____

2. What is the connection between earthquakes, volcanoes, and tectonic plates? Give evidence to support your answer.

____

____

____

____

____

Study the map on pages B20–B21. What are Earth's seven major tectonic plates? Make a chart in the space below that lists those tectonic plates and describes their locations by naming the continents or oceans with which each is associated.

ACTIVITY RECORD

Name ___________________________________ Date ___________

SEA-FLOOR SPREADING

Procedure

Record your inferences of how the movement of the strips of paper is like sea-floor spreading.

____

____

____

____

____

____

____

____

Analyze and Conclude

Write the answer to the question in your book on the lines below.

____

____

____

____

____

____

Name _________________________________ Date _________

BUILDING A MODEL OF THE OCEAN FLOOR

Procedure

Record your inference of what the clay, the shoebox, the shoebox lid, and the grid represent in your model.

____

____

____

____

____

____

____

Analyze and Conclude

Write the answers to the questions in your book on the lines below.

1. ____

____

____

2. ____

____

____

____

____

INVESTIGATE FURTHER

Name ___________________________ Date __________

Describe where the highest underwater mountains are located.

Infer how these mountainous features of the ocean floor might be related to Earth' plates.

Record the names of the sources you used in your research.

Name _______________________________________ Date __________

Mapping the Ocean Floor

Procedure

Make a chart in the space below to record the depth from the grid to the surface of the clay below each hole. Your chart should be like the examples shown on page B24. Remember, your chart must have places to record the depth to the clay beneath all the holes in the grid, each of which can be named with a letter and a number. For example, the first hole in the A row is *A1,* the third hole in the C row in *C3,* and so on. **Record all your measurements** on your chart.

Analyze and Conclude

Write the answers to the questions in your book on the lines below.

1. ____

____

____

2. ____

____

____

INVESTIGATE FURTHER

Name ________________________________ Date __________

Record the name, location, and depth of the deepest ocean trench.

Describe how oceanographers determined the depth of that trench.

Record the names of the sources you used in your research.

Name _______________________________________ Date ____________

INVESTIGATION 3

1. You are planning a TV program about the mysteries at the bottom of the sea. How would you explain sea-floor spreading to your viewers?

____

____

____

____

____

2. Describe some of the most important features you might find along a mid-ocean ridge. Explain how these features are formed.

____

____

____

____

____

Make a diagram in the space below that shows how the particles in the rock spreading from a mid-ocean ridge first point one way and then, when the Earth's magnetic field reverses, point the opposite way.

Name _______________________________________ Date ____________

CRACKED CRUST

What evidence supports the theory that continents move over time?

____

____

____

____

____

What is the theory of plate tectonics?

____

____

____

____

How are the locations of volcanoes and earthquakes related to Earth's tectonic plates?

____

____

____

How do scientists map the sea floor? Explain the process.

____

____

____

____

What does the sea floor tell us about plate tectonics?

____

____

____

____

Name _______________________________ Date __________

Think about what you learned in Chapter 1 when you answer the following questions.

1. What surprised you most as you read "Cracked Crust"?

____

____

____

____

____

2. How did reading the chapter change your understanding of how scientists use fossil evidence?

____

____

____

____

____

3. How did reading the chapter change what you think of when you hear about an earthquake or volcanic eruption?

____

____

____

____

____

4. What was the most difficult concept to understand in the chapter? What could you do to understand it better?

____

____

____

____

____

Name _______________________________ Date _______________

TECTONIC PLATES AND MOUNTAINS

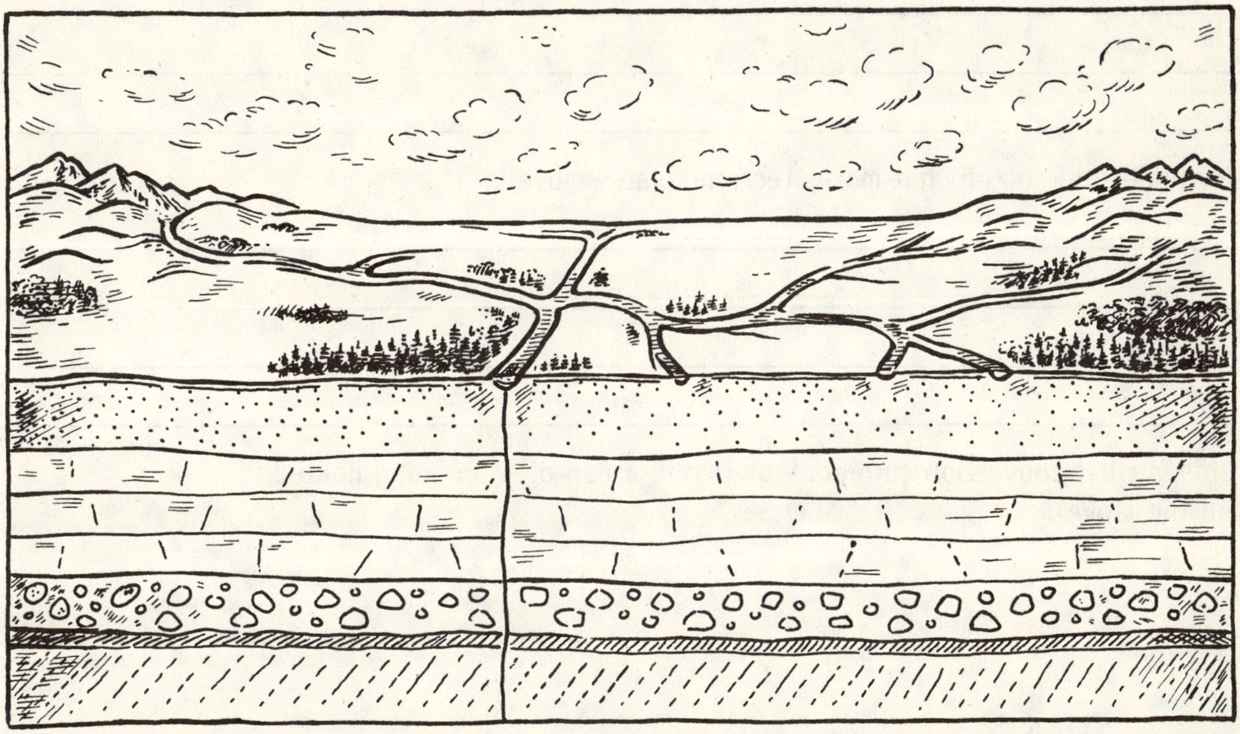

Can the movement of tectonic plates cause mountains to form? Draw how
you think this might happen.

Name _______________________________ Date __________

Dear Journal,

The structure of Earth includes these layers . . .

____

____

____

My understanding of what makes tectonic plates move is . . .

____

____

____

This is what convection currents look like in a pan of soup being heated
on the stove . . .

The mountains I've seen look like . . .

____

____

____

The way that mountains form is . . .

____

____

____

ACTIVITY RECORD

Name ___________________________ Date __________

THE CONVEYOR

Procedure

Write your predictions of what will happen when the holes in the carton are opened.

____

____

____

____

Record your observations of what happens when you pull the strings to peel the tape off the holes in the carton.

____

____

____

____

Write your hypothesis on how what occurs inside the aquarium is a model of the movement of material in Earth's crust and upper mantle.

____

____

____

____

Analyze and Conclude

Write the answers to the questions in your book on the lines below.

1. ____

____

____

____

____

Name ____ Date __________

2. ____

____

____

____

3. ____

____

____

____

____

INVESTIGATE FURFHER!
....
EXPERIMENT

Page B37

Predict what will happen if you floated a small piece of paper directly over the milk carton before you opened the holes.

Record your observations of what happens when you float a small piece of paper directly over the milk carton.

Compare your prediction with what actually happened.

INVESTIGATION 1

1. Can convergent and divergent plate boundaries be considered opposites?
Write a paragraph comparing these two kinds of plate boundaries.

____

____

____

____

____

____

2. Define the term *tectonic plate* and explain what might cause tectonic
plates to move.

____

____

____

Make a chart in the space below in which you can summarize your knowledge of types of plate boundaries. For each type, include the name, a
description of the movement of the plates involved, and an illustration.

Name _________________________________ Date ___________

COLLIDING PLATES

Procedure

Record your observations of what happens when you press one edge of
a sheet of cardboard firmly against a wall.

____

____

____

Write your predictions of what will happen when two plates meet.

____

____

____

____

Write your hypothesis of what happens when two plates meet at a convergent boundary. **Make a drawing** of your hypothesis in the space below.

____

____

____

____

ACTIVITY RECORD

Name _______________________________ Date _______________

Analyze and Conclude

Write the answers to the questions in your book on the lines below.

1. ____

____

____

____

2. ____

____

____

____

____

____

Name_________________________________ Date__________

UNIT PROJECT LINK

Identify some mountain systems around the world that are at convergent plate boundaries.

____

____

____

____

____

____

In the space below, record the data you collect from newspapers and magazines about earthquakes and volcanoes that have recently lifted mountains.

Share this information with your group.

Name _______________________________ Date __________

A BIG FENDER BENDER

Procedure

Record your hypothesis about what will happen when one continent bumps into another. **Make a drawing** of your hypothesis.

____

____

____

Write your prediction of what will happen if you place the sponges end to end and push them slowly into each other.

____

____

____

Record your observations of what happens when you place the sponges end to end and push them slowly into each other.

____

____

____

Name _______________________________ Date __________

Analyze and Conclude

Write the answers to the questions in your book on the lines below.

1. ____

   ____

   ____

2. ____

   ____

   ____

3. ____

   ____

   ____

Record which mountain range was thrust upward on the North American Plate when North America collided with North Africa to form part of Pangaea.

Describe what has happened to that mountain range since that time.

Record the names of the sources you used in your research.

INVESTIGATE FURTHER

Name ______________________________ Date __________

Sketch your model of how folded mountains form.

Sketch your model of how fault-block mountains form.

Name _______________________________________ Date _____________

INVESTIGATION 2

1. How are folded mountains like fault-block mountains? How are the
two kinds of mountains different? Write a paragraph comparing and
contrasting these kinds of mountains.

____

____

____

____

____

2. Describe the relationship between the collision of plates and the formation of mountains.

____

____

____

____

Make a chart in the space below to summarize your knowledge of the
four types of mountains. For each type, include the name, a brief description of how that type forms, and one or two examples.

Name ____ Date ____________

TECTONIC PLATES AND MOUNTAINS

Why do tectonic plates move?

____

____

____

____

What are the three types of plate boundaries? Describe the plates at each type.

____

____

____

____

____

____

What are the four basic types of mountains?

____

____

____

How does the motion of tectonic plates build mountains? What types of mountains does it build?

____

____

____

____

____

Name _________________________________ Date ___________

Think about what you learned in Chapter 2 when you answer the following questions.

1. What was the most interesting thing you learned as you read "Tectonic Plates and Mountains"?

____

____

____

____

____

2. What did you learn about tectonic plates that you still find hard to believe?

____

____

____

____

____

3. Where in the world would you like to visit to investigate ideas you read about in the chapter?

____

____

____

____

____

4. What concept did you find most difficult to understand as you read about the relationship between tectonic plates and mountains?

____

____

____

____

____

Name ____ Date _______________

SHAKE, RATTLE, AND ROLL

A strong earthquake has just struck the area. Draw how the inside of this house would look and how the land around the house might look.

Name _________________________________ Date _____________

Dear Journal,

I think that most earthquakes are caused by . . .

____

____

____

____

When I think of earthquakes, I think of . . .

____

____

____

____

____

When an earthquake occurs in an area, the ground itself can be described
as reacting in these ways . . .

____

____

____

____

I've heard that earthquakes are measured by . . .

____

____

____

Scientist are able to locate earthquakes by . . .

____

____

____

Name ___________________________________ Date _________

A MODEL OF SLIDING PLATES

Procedure

Write your prediction of what will happen if you hold the sandpaper surfaces tightly together and then try to slide the blocks past each other.

____

____

____

____

Record your observations of what happens when you slide the sandpaper-covered blocks past each other.

____

____

____

____

Record your explanation about how your moving the blocks might be like two tectonic plates passing each other.

____

____

____

____

Make a list of the places on your tectonic-plates map where plates are sliding past each other.

____

____

____

____

____

Name _________________________________ Date __________

Make a list of any features you find in those places that seem to be
related to the motion of plates.

____

____

____

____

Analyze and Conclude

Write the answers to the questions in your book on the lines below.

1. ____

____

____

____

____

2. ____

____

____

____

____

Name _________________________________ Date _____________

Describe what you see, feel, and hear as you slide one brick over another.

Describe what you see, feel, and hear as you slide one smooth rock over another.

Infer how the movement of tectonic plates might be similar to your movements of bricks and rocks.

Describe what you found out about animals' sensitivity to changes that occur before an earthquake.

Do you think people could use such animal behavior as a warning sign for an earthquake?

Name ____ Date ___________

INVESTIGATION 1

1. You are writing a news report on an earthquake that has just occurred. Tell your readers where and why the quake occurred, which plates were involved, and how severe it was.

____

____

____

____

____

____

____

____

2. Explain how the movement of tectonic plates and the occurrence of earthquakes are related.

____

____

____

____

Make a list in the space below of what scientists watch for in trying to predict earthquakes.

Name _______________________________________ Date ____________

SHAKE IT!

Procedure

Write your predictions of what will happen when you shake the bowl of sand with the block of wood standing in it.

____

____

____

Record your observations of what happens when you shake the bowl of sand with the block of wood standing in it.

____

____

____

Write your predictions of what will happen when you shake the bowl of wet sand with the block of wood standing in it.

____

____

____

Record your observations of what happens when you shake the bowl of wet sand with the block of wood standing in it.

____

____

____

Write your predictions of what will happen when you shake the bowl of gelatin with the block of wood standing in it.

____

____

____

Name _______________________________________ Date ___________

Record your observations of what happens when you shake the bowl of gelatin with the block of wood standing on it.

____

____

____

Analyze and Conclude

Write the answers to the questions in your book on the lines below.

1. ____

____

____

____

____

2. ____

____

____

____

3. ____

____

____

____

UNIT B

Name____ Date____________

UNIT PROJECT LINK

Describe where Anchorage is located in Alaska.

____

____

____

Describe where Crescent City is located in California.

____

____

____

Record your computation of the distance the tsunami traveled.

____

From your study of the earthquake map on page B17, which North American coastlines do you think might experience tsunamis?

____

____

____

What do you think people could do along that coastline to prevent damage or save their lives when tsunamis occur.

____

____

____

____

____

Share this information with your group.

Name _______________________________________ Date ______________

INVESTIGATION 2

1. Describe and make drawings of the changes taking place in Earth's crust during an earthquake. Explain the forces that caused these changes.

2. What is the connection between a fault and the production of an earthquake? Give a well-known example of such a connection.

____

____

____

____

Make a chart in the space below to summarize your understanding of types of faults. For each type, list its name, describe the forces that are acting on it, and describe the movement of the slabs of rock.

Name _______________________________ Date _____________

SHAKE IT HARDER!

Procedure

Write your predictions of what will be shown on the seismogram if you shake the table gently.

____

____

____

____

Analyze and Conclude

Write the answers to the questions in your book on the lines below.

1. ____

____

____

2. ____

____

____

3. ____

____

____

____

Name _______________________________________ Date ___________

Describe how well the seismograph works if you shake the desk in the same direction as the paper is being pulled.

Compare your results with a real seismograph.

Infer the connection between the length of strings and the working of the seismograph.

Name _______________________________________ Date ___________

LOCATING EARTHQUAKES

Procedure

Make a table in the space below like the one on page B70. Then record
the results of your calculations in the last column.

Record the distance from Tucson to the epicenter of the quake.

____

Record the distance from Billings to the epicenter of the quake.

____

Record the distance from Houston to the epicenter of the quake.

____

Analyze and Conclude

Write the answers to the questions in your book on the lines below.

1. ____

____

____

2. ____

____

Name _______________________________________ Date ___________

3. ____
____
____
____

4. ____
____
____
____

INVESTIGATE FURTHER!

TAKE ACTION

Page B71

Record the location of the office of the U.S. Geological Survey with which you made contact.

Describe your visit or call.

Record the information about locating earthquakes you learned.

Name ____ Date ___________

BE AN ARCHITECT

Procedure

Make a drawing of your design of a high-rise building that will not tip over in an earthquake.

Record your standard for when a building is considered earthquake-proof.

____

____

Write your prediction of how well your building will withstand an earth-quake.

____

____

____

Name _________________________ Date _________

Record your observations of how well your building withstood the earthquake.

____

____

____

____

Record your comparisons of your results with those of other groups in your class.

____

____

____

____

____

____

Analyze and Conclude

Write the answers to the questions in your book on the lines below.

1. ____

____

____

2. ____

____

____

____

3. ____

____

____

Name _________________________________ Date _____________

Draw the redesign of your building in the space below. With labels, point out what features have been redesigned.

Describe ways you think tall buildings could be made earthquake-proof.

Describe what you learned about early seismographs.

Compare the early seismograph you described with a modern seismograph.

Record the names of the sources you used in your research.

Name ____________________________ Date __________

INVESTIGATION 3

1. Compare the effects of an earthquake in which the focus is under the ocean with one in which the focus is under the land.

____

____

____

____

____

2. Nearly everyone knows that earthquakes can be dangerous. Explain why some people still choose to live in earthquake-prone areas.

____

____

____

____

In the space below, draw two waves: a wave that represents a tsunami in the open ocean, and a wave that represents a tsunami near the shore. Label the waves you draw.

CHAPTER WRAP-UP

Name _______________________________________ Date ______________

SHAKE, RATTLE, AND ROLL

What causes earthquakes and how can they be compared?

____
____
____
____

What happens to Earth's crust during an earthquake?

____
____
____
____

What is the difference between the focus and the epicenter of an earth-quake?

____
____
____

How are earthquakes located and measured?

____
____
____
____

What is a tsunami and what causes it?

____
____
____

Name ______________________________ Date __________

Think about what you learned in Chapter 3 when you answer the following questions.

1. What was the most interesting thing you learned about earthquakes as you read "Shake, Rattle, and Roll"?

____

____

____

____

____

2. What did you learn about earthquakes that surprised you most?

____

____

____

____

____

3. Now that you know about earthquakes, would you consider living in an earthquake-prone area? Explain your answer.

____

____

____

____

____

4. What concept did you find most difficult to understand as you read the chapter?

____

____

____

____

____

Use with pages B82–B83.

CHAPTER PREVIEW

CHAPTER 4

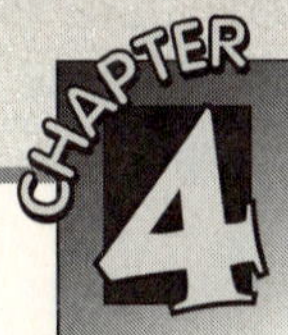

Name ______________________ Date __________

Volcanoes

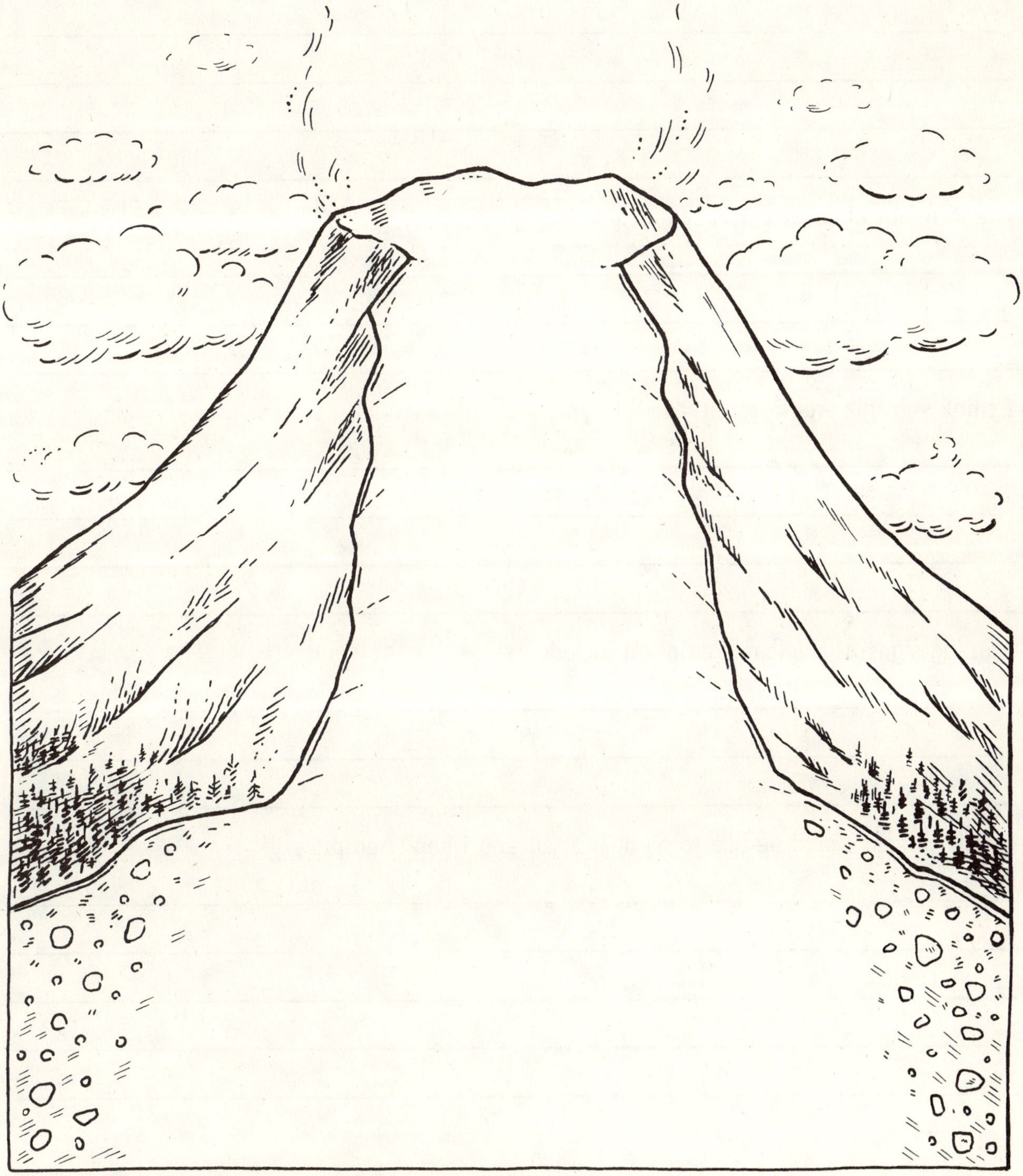

A volcano erupts! What do you think it looks like inside and outside the volcano? Draw your ideas.

CHAPTER PREVIEW

Name ___________________________ Date __________

Dear Journal,

Most volcanoes on Earth can be found in these areas . . .

____

____

____

The different kinds of volcanoes include . . .

____

____

____

I think volcanic eruptions are caused by . . .

____

____

____

____

Warning signs of a volcanic eruption include . . .

____

____

____

This is what it would be like to be near a volcano when it erupts . . .

____

____

____

____

Name _________________________________ Date _________

WORLDWIDE ERUPTIONS

Procedure

Make a chart in the space below to record data about volcanic eruptions during a six-month period in the last two years. In your chart you will need places to **record:** (1) the date of the eruption, (2) the name of the volcano, (3) the location, (4) the volcano's relationship to a tectonic plate, and (5) a description of the eruption.

Name _________________________________ Date ___________

Make a chart in the space below like the chart you made on the previous page to record new volcanic activity and eruptions as they occur.

Analyze and Conclude

Write the answers to the questions in your book on the lines below.

1. ____

2. ____

   ____

3. ____

   ____

   ____

4. ____

   ____

   ____

Name _______________________________ Date ___________

Record the names of islands you found are at the same locations as mid-ocean ridges.

Describe any volcanic activity on these islands, including what type of volcanoes are there.

Record the names of the sources you used in your research.

Describe how destructive the eruption on Heimaey was.

Describe a way the eruption benefitted the island.

Compare the eruption on Heimaey with that on Surtsey.

Name _______________________________ Date __________

INVESTIGATION 1

1. Describe how most volcanoes form.

____

____

2. Make a chart that compares and contrasts cinder cones, shield volcanoes, and composite cones. In your chart, include a sketch of each type of volcano. Label the parts of each volcano.

Describe how volcanoes are classified on the basis of how often eruptions occur.

____

____

____

____

ACTIVITY RECORD

CHAPTER 4

Name ___________________________ Date ___________

VOLCANOES YOU CAN EAT!

Procedure

Record your observations of the top surface of the oatmeal as it cooks.

____

____

____

____

____

Analyze and Conclude

Write the answers to the questions in your book on the lines below.

1. ____

____

____

____

2. ____

____

____

____

Name_____________________________________ Date___________

UNIT PROJECT LINK

Identify islands in the Ring of Fire that have been created by volcanic activity.

____

____

____

____

____

Predict where future volcanic islands might rise out of the ocean.
Explain your reasoning.

____

____

____

____

Describe where you think your island will emerge.

____

____

____

Draw a picture of your future island paradise.

Share this information with your group.

INVESTIGATE FURTHER

Name _______________________________ Date _____________

Describe the location of Mount Mayon.

Describe this volcano, how you think it formed, and what kind of volcano it is.

Record the years you discovered that Mount Mayon has erupted.

Name ______________________________________ Date __________

INVESTIGATION 2

1. Using Mount Pinatubo as your example, explain how volcanic eruptions can have long-term effects on the planet.

____

____

____

____

2. Describe some of the events that may occur and some measurements that may be taken to alert scientists to a coming volcanic eruption.

____

____

____

____

____

____

Imagine that you are a TV reporter for one of the major networks when Mount Pinatubo erupts. You're on the island of Luzon, near enough to the eruption to smell the ash. With Pinatubo in the background, the camera light flashes. You're on! Tell the folks at home about this eruption—why it happened, what were the warning signs, and what it's like now.

____

____

____

____

____

____

____

____

ACTIVITY RECORD

CHAPTER 4

Name _______________________________ Date _____________

How Hawaii Formed

Procedure

Record your measurements of the distance between the center of the island of Hawaii and the center of each of the other major islands.

____

____

____

____

Record the youngest island and the oldest island of the island group.

____

____

Make a chart in the space below that shows the distances between the island of Hawaii and the other islands as well as the age differences between the island of Hawaii and the other islands.

ACTIVITY RECORD

Use with pages B100–B101.

Name ________________________ Date __________

Analyze and Conclude

Write the answers to the questions in your book on the lines below.

1. ____
____
____
____
____
____
____

2. ____
____

3. ____
____

4. ____
____

5. ____
____
____
____

INVESTIGATE FURTHER

Name ___________________________________ Date __________

Describe the bend you see between the Hawaiian Islands and the Emperor Seamount chain.

Infer what this bend means.

Name _________________________________ Date ___________

INVESTIGATION 3

1. Volcanoes occur on Earth's surface—the crust. Yet scientists study volcanoes to find out about the planet's mantle. Explain why.

____

____

____

____

____

2. Using the Hawaiian Islands as an example, describe how volcanic islands can occur in places other than at the boundaries of tectonic plates.

____

____

____

____

Make a flow chart in the space below to explain the probable formation of Africa's highest peak, Mt. Kilimanjaro.

CHAPTER WRAP-UP

Name ____________________________________ Date __________

VOLCANOES
. . . .

Where do volcanoes occur, and how are they classified?

____

____

____

____

____

How do volcanic eruptions affect Earth?

____

____

____

How did the Hawaiian Islands form?

____

____

Think back to the drawing you made of the erupting volcano on page 99.
In the space below, make another drawing that shows your new knowledge of the structure of a volcano. Label its parts.

Name _______________________________________ Date ____________

Think about what you learned in Chapter 4 when you answer the following questions.

1. What interested you most as you read "Volcanoes"?

____

____

____

____

____

2. Where would you like to visit in the world to further investigate the nature of volcanoes? Explain why.

____

____

____

____

____

3. What did you find most surprising about volcanoes?

____

____

____

____

____

4. What else would you like to learn about volcanoes and their eruptions? What could you do to find out?

____

____

____

____

____

Name_______________________________________ Date__________

UNIT PROJECT WRAP-UP

Think about the guide, Preparing for an Earthquake and for Volcanic Activity, you helped develop for the Unit Project Big Event. Describe the part of the guide you felt most proud to have helped prepare.

____

____

____

____

You've researched areas that have high frequencies of earthquakes. What three preventative measures described in the guide do you think would be most important for people in such areas to follow?

____

____

____

____

What three preventative measures described in the guide do you think would be most important for people near volcanoes to follow?

____

____

____

____

If you were to distribute this guide around the world to help peo-ple prepare for earthquake and volcanic activity, what else would you like to include in it?

____

____

____

UNIT C

Name_______________________________________ Date___________

THE NATURE OF MATTER

In Unit C you'll learn about the characteristics and kinds of matter as well as how matter changes. In the Unit Project Big Event, you'll put on a magic show that will demonstrate your knowledge of matter, its properties, and its behavior. What do you think matter is?

____

____

____

____

Do you think that when magicians make objects disappear they are really doing away with or destroying matter? Explain your answer.

____

____

____

____

____

____

____

Describe an amazing magic trick you've seen in which matter was "changed" in form or made to "disappear."

____

____

____

____

____

____

____

Name_________________________________ Date__________

UNIT PREVIEW

What do you know about matter and how it changes? What more
would you like to learn? Write your ideas on the lines below.

Name _________________________________ Date ___________

CHARACTERISTICS OF MATTER

All materials can be classified into three major forms, or states. On the right, you see a scene with water vapor, an invisible gas, condensing to a cloud. Draw two more scenes to picture water in its two familiar forms.

Name _______________________________ Date __________

Dear Journal,

Some of the ways that we measure matter include . . .

____

____

____

____

____

I think a kind of material will float in water if . . .

____

____

____

____

____

The three forms, or states, of matter are . . .

____

____

____

____

____

Increasing the temperature of a material has this effect . . .

____

____

____

____

____

ACTIVITY RECORD

Name ____ Date ____________

A MATTER OF MASS

Procedure

Record your observations of the sizes and shapes of the three containers, by looking at them and not picking them up.

____

____

____

____

Record your arrangement of the containers, from heaviest to lightest, based on the way the containers feel.

____

____

____

Make a chart in the space below like the one shown on page C6 in which you can record the mass and contents of each container.

Name ________________________________ Date __________

Analyze and Conclude

Write the answers to the questions in your book on the lines below.

1. ____
____
____

2. ____
____
____
____

3. ____
____
____
____
____

Name _______________________________________ Date _____________

A MATTER OF SPACE

Procedure

Write your prediction of which material, cotton or an equal mass of sand, will take up more space if placed in containers.

____

____

____

Record your measurement of the mass of the bag of cotton.

____

____

Record your measurement of how many milliliters of sand are in the bag.

____

____

Record your measurement of how many milliliters of cotton are in the plastic bag.

____

____

Analyze and Conclude

Write the answers to the questions in your book on the lines below.

1. ____

____

2. ____

____

3. ____

____

____

Name _______________________________________ Date _____________

CHECKING FOR PURITY

Procedure

Record your inferences about the mass and volume of the ball and the cube.

____

____

____

Record your measurements of the mass of the ball and of the cube.

____

____

Record your measurement of the volume of water in the measuring cup when you have filled it half full.

____

Record your measurement of the volume of water once you have placed the ball in the cup.

____

Record your measurement of the volume of water once you have placed the cube in the cup.

____

____

Analyze and Conclude

Write the answers to the questions in your book on the lines below.

1. ____

____

2. ____

____

Name _______________________________________ Date ____________

3. ____

____

____

4. ____

____

____

Describe the design of your experiment to find the density of an object that floats in water.

Record the results of your experiment.

Name _________________________________ Date __________

INVESTIGATION 1

1. Explain why density provides a more useful description of a material than does either mass or volume by itself.

____

____

____

2. You have a cube and a sphere, each with a mass of 10 g. The cube floats in water; the sphere does not. What can you infer about the volume of each object? Explain the reasoning behind your inference.

____

____

____

____

____

Make flow charts to show the methods you would use to find the volume of (1) a wooden rectangular block and (2) a child's small toy truck.

Name _________________________________ Date ___________

ALWAYS ROOM FOR MORE

Procedure

Record your inference about whether the jar has room for more matter once you have filled it to the brim with marbles.

____

____

____

Record your inference about whether the jar has room for more matter once you have added sand to the jar of marbles.

____

____

____

Record your observations of what happens when you add a spoonful of sugar to a second jar of water and stir.

____

____

Analyze and Conclude

Write the answers to the questions in your book on the lines below.

1. ____

____

____

2. ____

____

3. ____

____

____

____

Name _______________________________________ Date ___________

4. ____

____

____

5.

Predict what will happen when you repeat steps 1–3
of the activity using modeling clay instead of marbles
in step 1.

Record your observations of what happened when you used
modeling clay instead of marbles.

Infer why there was a difference in results when you used modeling clay instead of marbles.

ACTIVITY RECORD

Name ________________________________ Date __________

RACING LIQUIDS

Procedure

Write your prediction of which paper strip the water will move through most quickly.

____

____

Analyze and Conclude

Write the answers to the questions in your book on the lines below.

1. ____

____

2. ____

____

____

____

3.

4. ____

____

____

CHAPTER 1

Name _________________________________ Date __________

INVESTIGATION 2

1. Why do solids have a definite shape while liquids and gases do not?

____

____

____

____

2. Iron expands when it is heated. Draw a sketch of how the particles of a piece of iron might look at 10°C and at 50°C.

Complete the chart below to summarize your understanding of states of matter. (In the middle column, write "yes" or "no" for each state.)

State	Definite Shape?	Description of Particles

ACTIVITY RECORD

Name ____ Date _____________

COOLING RACE

Procedure

Make a chart in the space below like the one shown on page C22. **Record** the temperature of the water in each jar under Start in your chart. Then at three-minute intervals **record the temperature** of the water in each jar.

Analyze and Conclude

Write the answers to the questions in your book on the lines below.

1. ____

____

2. ____

3. ____

____

____

4. ____

____

5. ____

____

____

Name _________________________________ Date _________

Predict the changes that would occur if you added an equal number of ice cubes to both a glass of cold water and a glass of warm water.

Record your observations of what occurred when you tried this experiment.

Infer why there was a difference in the speed at which the ice melted in the two glasses.

Name ____ Date ___________

SPEEDING UP CHANGE

Procedure

Write your prediction of what will happen to the two drops of water in the dish placed in direct sunlight and the dish placed in a cool, shaded spot.

____

____

Record your observations of what happens when you place the two dishes in different spots.

____

____

Make a list of your suggestions of ways to make a drop of water evaporate faster.

____

____

____

Record your observations in the chart below for each of the techniques you try in making the drop of water evaporate faster.

Technique	Results

Name ___________________________ Date __________

Analyze and Conclude

Write the answers to the questions in your book on the lines below.

1. ____

   ____

   ____

2. ____

   ____

   ____

   ____

   ____

   ____

   ____

   ____

3. ____

   ____

   ____

UNIT
C

Name_________________________________ Date__________

UNIT PROJECT LINK

Describe the trick you selected to master for the magic show.

____
____
____
____
____
____

Why did you select the trick you did?

____
____
____
____
____

Explain how and why the trick works. Use your understanding of
matter to tell the reasons for what happens.

____
____
____
____
____
____
____

Share this information with your group.

Name _______________________________________ Date ____________

INVESTIGATION 3

1. Describe the changes that take place in a sample of water as it changes from water vapor to liquid water to ice.

____

____

____

____

____

____

2. If you hold an ice cube in one hand and a hot muffin in the other, one hand feels cold and the other feels hot. Explain these feelings in terms of movement of heat.

____

____

____

____

____

Make a drawing that shows how the transfer of heat energy changes the state of water in a pan on a stovetop burner. Use labels and arrows to make your drawing clear.

Name ___________________________ Date ___________

CHARACTERISTICS OF MATTER

What is matter and how can it be described?

____

____

____

____

____

What makes up matter?

____

____

____

____

What two things determine the state matter is in?

____

____

____

____

How does adding or taking away energy affect matter?

____

____

____

____

____

Name _______________________________________ Date ____________

Think about what you learned in Chapter 1 when you answer the following questions.

1. What did you learn in reading "Characteristics of Matter" that most changes your way of looking at the natural world?

____

____

____

____

2. What was the most difficult concept to understand in the chapter? What could you do to understand it better?

____

____

____

____

____

____

3. What was the most useful thing you learned in the chapter?

____

____

____

____

4. What was something you learned in reading the chapter that you had always wondered about?

____

____

____

____

Name ____ Date _____________

KINDS OF MATTER

What are the ways that matter can be combined? A mixture is one way.
Make a mixture in the bowl that would be good to eat by using the
ingredients around the edge of the bowl.

Name _______________________________ Date _____________

Dear Journal,

The smallest particle of a substance that can still be recognized as that substance is called . . .

____

____

These are some chemical symbols I know . . .

____

____

____

____

____

____

I think a mixture is different from a chemical compound in that . . .

____

____

____

____

____

____

A liquid mixture that I like to drink is a mixture of . . .

____

____

____

Name _______________________________________ Date _____________

TESTING YOUR METAL

Procedure

Make a list of the properties of aluminum and copper while examining
the samples of each.

____

____

____

____

____

____

Make a list of things you could do to change the samples of aluminum
and copper.

____

____

____

____

Record your observations for each of your ways to change the metals
that you carry out.

____

____

____

____

____

____

Name _______________________________ Date _________

Analyze and Conclude

Write the answers to the questions in your book on the lines below.

1. ____

____

____

____

____

2. ____

____

____

____

CHAPTER 2

Name _______________________________________ Date ___________

A CHANGE FOR THE WETTER

Procedure

Make a sketch of a sugar grain from what you observe with the hand lens.

Record your observations of the sugar and the glass square as you heated the sugar in the spoon.

____

____

____

____

Analyze and Conclude

Write the answers to the questions in your book on the lines below.

1. ____

____

2. ____

____

3. ____

____

Name______________________________________ Date__________

UNIT PROJECT LINK

Describe the trick you selected to work on with your group.

____

____

____

____

____

____

____

Why do you want to master this trick?

____

____

____

____

____

Explain how and why the trick works. Use your understanding of
matter to tell the reasons for what happens.

____

____

____

____

____

____

____

Share this information with your group.

Name _________________________________ Date _________

INVESTIGATION 1

1. What do elements and compounds have in common? How do they differ?

____

____

____

____

____

2. The chemical formula for carbon dioxide is CO_2. The formula for sulfur trioxide is SO_3. The formula for carbon tetrachloride is CCl_4. From the information in the formulas, infer the meanings of the prefixes *di-*, *tri-*, and *tetra-*.

____

____

____

For each of the chemical formulas below, write how many atoms of each element a single molecule (or unit) of the compound contains.

Fe_2O_3 (iron rust) ___________________________________

____

SnO_2 (jewelers' putty) ___________________________________

____

NH_3 (ammonia) ___________________________________

____

$PbCrO_4$ (chrome yellow) ___________________________________

____

$Na_2Si_4O_9$ (water glass) ___________________________________

____

$C_6H_5NO_2$ (nitrobenzene) ___________________________________

____

Name ______________________________ Date __________

WORKING WITH MIXTURES

Procedure

Write your prediction about whether the properties of any of the materials in the jar will be changed by being mixed together.

____

____

____

Write a description of the contents of the jar after you have examined them with a hand lens.

____

____

____

Write a description of a way you could separate the parts of the mixture in the jar.

____

____

____

Record your plan for separating the sand-gravel mixture.

____

____

____

____

Record your plan for separating the sand-gravel-sugar mixture.

____

____

____

____

ACTIVITY RECORD

CHAPTER 2

Name _______________________________________ Date ____________

Analyze and Conclude

Write the answers to the questions in your book on the lines below.

1. ____

____

____

2. ____

____

____

____

3. ____

____

____

____

Describe the plan you've made to separate the mixture of sand and iron filings.

Infer from the results of your experiment whether the properties of either the sand or the iron filings were changed when the substances were combined.

Name _______________________________________ Date ____________

RACING COLORS

Procedure

Write your prediction of what will happen as water moves up the cone
and past the marker spots.

____

____

____

____

Record your observations of what happens as water moves up the cone
and past the marker spots.

____

____

____

____

____

Analyze and Conclude

Write the answers to the questions in your book on the lines below.

1. ____

____

____

2. ____

____

____

ACTIVITY RECORD

Name _________________________________ Date ___________

A MIXED-UP STATE

Procedure

Write your prediction of how the cornstarch will change if you add water to it.

____

____

____

____

Record your observations of the material you have created by adding the colored water to the cornstarch.

____

____

____

____

____

Analyze and Conclude

Write the answers to the questions in your book on the lines below.

1. ____

____

____

2. ____

____

____

3. ____

____

____

CHAPTER 2

Name _______________________________ Date __________

INVESTIGATION 2

1. Explain why a mixture is not a substance and cannot be represented by a chemical formula.

____

____

____

____

2. Suppose you had a mixture of iron pellets, pebbles, and small wood spheres, all about the same size. How would you separate this mixture?

____

____

____

____

Complete the chart below to summarize your understanding of the differences between mixtures and chemical compounds.

	Substances keep original properties?	Separated by physical means?	Examples
Mixtures			
Compounds			

ACTIVITY RECORD

CHAPTER 2

Name ___________________________ Date ___________

MIXING SOLIDS INTO LIQUIDS

Procedure

Write your prediction of the conditions in which a sugar cube will dissolve most quickly. Choose from among the conditions listed in the chart on page C53.

____

____

____

Make a chart in the space below like the one on page C53 to record the times it takes sugar cubes to dissolve in water under several conditions.

Analyze and Conclude

Write the answers to the questions in your book on the lines below.

1. ____

____

2. ____

____

Name ____ Date ___________

3. ____

____

4. ____

____

5. ____

____

____

____

____

____

INVESTIGATE FURTHER!

EXPERIMENT

Page C53

Infer why you think ocean water is salty. Where does the salt (dissolved minerals) come from?

Describe the design of a method you think could be used to get the salt out of ocean water.

ACTIVITY RECORD

Name ___________________________ Date __________

TO MIX OR NOT TO MIX

Procedure

Record your observations of what happens to the liquids in the bottle when you shake it and then stand it on the table.

____

____

____

____

Record your observations of what happens to the liquids when you turn the bottle upside down and hold it that way.

____

____

____

____

Analyze and Conclude

Write the answers to the questions in your book on the lines below.

1. ____

____

____

2. ____

____

____

3. ____

____

4. ____

____

ACTIVITY RECORD

Use with page C55.

Name _______________________________ Date __________

MAKING WATER WETTER

Procedure

Record your observations of the shape and behavior of a drop from one of the two colored liquids.

____

____

____

____

____

____

Record your observations of the shape and behavior of a drop from the other of the two colored liquids.

____

____

____

____

____

____

Record your observations of the shape and behavior of a drop of uncolored water.

____

____

____

____

____

ACTIVITY RECORD

Name ___________________________ Date __________

Analyze and Conclude

Write the answers to the questions in your book on the lines below.

1. ____
____
____
____

2. ____
____
____
____

3. ____
____

4. ____
____
____

Name _______________________________ Date _____________

INVESTIGATION 3

1. Explain why salad dressing is not a solution.

____
____
____
____

2. Why is an alloy both a mixture and a solution?

____
____
____

Make a labeled drawing to show how a solute and a solvent form a solution.

CHAPTER WRAP-UP

Name _______________________________________ Date _____________

KINDS OF MATTER

How can matter be classified? Make a word map that shows the relationships among the different kinds of matter.

What is the difference between an element and a compound?

____

____

____

____

What is a mixture?

____

____

____

Describe a mixture of sugar and water.

____

____

____

Name ____ Date ___________

Think about what you learned in Chapter 2 when you answer the following questions.

1. What was the most interesting thing you learned as you read "Kinds of Matter"?

____

____

____

____

____

2. Think back to the tossed salad you drew on page 139. Tell what kind of mixture you drew and give reasons for your answer.

____

____

____

____

____

3. What was the most difficult concept for you to learn in the chapter? What could you do to make it clearer to you?

____

____

____

____

____

____

Name ______________________________ Date __________

How Matter Changes

Do the materials in the first box suggest that something will happen? In the middle box, draw what you think will happen. In the final box, draw the result, after everything is over.

Name _______________________ Date _______

Dear Journal,

These are some of the chemical reactions I've observed or know about . . .

____

____

____

____

In a chemical reaction, substances . . .

____

____

____

____

I've seen acids used to . . .

____

____

____

____

I think the work that chemists do includes . . .

____

____

____

____

Name _______________________________________ Date ___________

BALLOON BLOWER

Procedure

Record your observations of what happens when you hold the balloon
so that the baking soda falls into the bottle containing vinegar.

____

____

____

____

____

____

Analyze and Conclude

Write the answers to the questions in your book on the lines below.

1. ____

____

____

____

____

2. ____

____

____

____

3. ____

____

____

Name _______________________________________ Date _______________

Record what you discovered baking soda contains.

Describe what baking soda does when a food containing it is cooked.

List some kinds of foods that include baking soda as an ingredient.

CHAPTER 3

Name _________________________________ Date __________

MAKING A FIRE EXTINGUISHER

Procedure

Record your observations of what happens to the flame when you insert the burning match first into the jar containing baking soda and then into the jar containing vinegar.

____

____

____

Write your description of what happens when you carefully pour the vinegar into the jar containing baking soda.

____

____

____

Record your observations of what happens when you insert the tip of the burning match into the jar containing the vinegar and baking soda.

____

____

____

Analyze and Conclude

Write the answers to the questions in your book on the lines below.

1. ____

____

2. ____

____

Name ____ Date ___________

SOLIDS FROM LIQUIDS

Procedure

Record your observations of the unknown liquids *A* and *B*.

____

____

____

____

Record your observations of changes in the mixture after five minutes.

____

____

____

____

Analyze and Conclude

Write the answers to the questions in your book on the lines below.

1. ____

____

____

2. ____

____

____

3. ____

____

____

INVESTIGATION CLOSE

Name ____ Date ____________

INVESTIGATION 1

1. How does heating sugar in a spoon differ from dissolving it in a cup of hot water?

____

____

____

____

____

2. Suppose two neutrons escape the nucleus of an atom. What effect would this event have on the atomic number of and total electric charge on the atom? Explain your answer.

____

____

____

____

Remember that an atom usually has the same number of electrons as it does protons. Some atoms also have the same number of neutrons as protons. Using information from the periodic table on pages C36 and C37, make three drawings in the space below: (1) a Bohr model of a lithium atom, (2) an electron cloud model of a lithium atom, and (3) a Bohr model of a positive lithium ion.

Name _________________________________ Date __________

CABBAGE-JUICE SCIENCE

Procedure

Make a chart in the space below like the one on page C79 in which you can record your observations when you add drops of various materials to jars containing red cabbage juice. Make the chart big enough to record the results of seven tests.

Record in your chart any changes you see when you add vinegar to jar 1, lemon juice to jar 2, baking soda to jar 3, and powdered lime to jar 4.

Write your prediction of what changes will occur when you add pineapple juice to red cabbage juice in a clean jar.

____

____

Record in your chart any changes you see when you add pineapple juice to red cabbage juice in a clean jar.

Write your prediction of what changes will occur when you add liquid soap to red cabbage juice in a clean jar.

____

____

Record in your chart any changes you see when you add liquid soap to red cabbage juice in a clean jar.

Name _____________________________________ Date _____________

Write your prediction of what changes will occur when you add vinegar
to jar 3, in which you have already added baking soda.

____

____

Record in your chart any changes you see when you add vinegar to jar
3, in which you have already added baking soda.

Analyze and Conclude

Write the answers to the questions in your book on the lines below.

1. ____

____

2. ____

____

3. ____

____

4. ____

____

Record your observations for the liquids you tested.

Classify the liquids you tested into two groups, based on how
they react with the cabbage-juice indicator.

Name _______________________________________ Date _____________

THE LITMUS TEST

Procedure

Make a chart in the space below like the one shown on page C80. In your chart, **record** your tests of the three liquids with red and blue litmus paper.

Analyze and Conclude

Write the answers to the questions in your book on the lines below.

1. ____

____

____

2. ____

____

____

3. ____

____

____

UNIT PROJECT LINK

Name____ Date__________

Unit Project Link

Describe the trick you selected to work on with your group.

____

____

____

____

____

____

____

Why do you want to master this trick?

____

____

____

____

____

Explain how and why the trick works. Use your understanding of matter to tell the reasons for what happens.

____

____

____

____

____

____

Share this information with your group.

Name _________________________________ Date _________

INVESTIGATION 2

1. What properties do acids and bases have in common? How are they different?

____

____

____

____

____

____

2. You test the pH of a solution and find it to be 11. What effect would this solution have on litmus paper? How would you neutralize this solution?

____

____

____

____

Make a flow chart that explains the formation and effects of acid rain.

Name _______________________________ Date ____________

TESTING A TABLET

Procedure

Record your observations of any properties of the tablet you can see
just by looking at it and handling it.

____

____

____

____

Record your observations of what happens when you add one piece of
the tablet to a test tube half full of water.

____

____

____

Write a description of what you feel when you hold the bottom of the test
tube in one hand and cover the opening of the test tube with your thumb.

____

____

____

____

Write a description of what you see when you examine the small pieces
of the tablet with a hand lens.

____

____

____

Record your observations of what happens when you dip the lighted
match into the beaker above the surface of the liquid.

____

____

Name _______________________________ Date _______________

Analyze and Conclude

Write the answers to the questions in your book on the lines below.

1. ____

2. ____

3. ____

4. ____

INVESTIGATE FURTHER

Name ____ Date ____________

Describe the design of your own experiment using the remaining piece of the tablet.

Record the results of your experiment.

Name _________________________________ Date __________

MYSTERY POWDERS

Procedure

Make a chart in the space below like the one on page C88. Use the headings *Appearance, Water, Vinegar,* and *Iodine* across the top and list the letters of the 6 mystery powders down the side. In your chart, **record** how each powder looks and the results of each of the tests you do.

Name ___________________________________ Date ___________

Analyze and Conclude

Write the answers to the questions in your book on your chart and on
the lines below.

1. ____

____

2. ____

____

____

Record the powder you used in your experiment.

Record the observations of your classmates as they tested your
mystery powder.

Identify which of the six mystery powders your powder was most
like.

Name _______________________________ Date ___________

"Slime" Time

Procedure

Write a description of each of the materials you are going to mix
together, listing as many properties of each as you can.

____

____

____

____

____

Record your observations of any changes in the appearance of the mixture as you gradually stir in the white powder.

____

____

____

____

____

Analyze and Conclude

Write the answers to the questions in your book on the lines below.

1. ____

____

2. ____

____

____

3. ____

____

____

INVESTIGATE FURTHER

CHAPTER 3

Name _________________________________ Date __________

Sketch the polymer model you made.

Describe the properties of the polymer you modeled.

Name _______________________________________ Date ___________

INVESTIGATION 3

1. Compare and contrast synthesis and analysis.

____

____

____

____

2. Why are there so many more compounds of carbon than of any other element? Use your knowledge of elements and the periodic table to hypothesize which group of elements forms the fewest compounds.

____

____

____

____

____

In the space below, draw a cartoon for each type of chemical reaction. Your cartoons could be of anything, as long as they put across the basic concept of each type of reaction. Label your cartoons *Synthesis, Decomposition, Single Replacement,* and *Double Replacement.*

Name ___________________________________ Date ___________

HOW MATTER CHANGES

Describe the difference between a physical change and a chemical change.

____

____

____

____

____

What is the law of conservation of mass?

____

____

____

What are acids, bases, and salts?

____

____

____

____

____

____

What are the two large categories of things chemists do?

____

____

____

____

What are the four types of chemical reactions?

____

____

____

Name _________________________________ Date __________

Think about what you learned in Chapter 3 when you answer the following questions.

1. What did you learn as you read "How Matter Changes" that you've always wondered about?

____

____

____

____

____

2. What did you learn about in reading the chapter that gave you a better understanding of something you already knew about?

____

____

____

____

____

3. Describe something you learned that you could tell to impress an adult in your family.

____

____

____

____

____

4. What else would you like to know about how matter changes? What could you do to find out?

____

____

____

____

____

UNIT
C

UNIT WRAP-UP

Name_______________________________________ Date__________

UNIT PROJECT WRAP-UP

Think about the magic show you helped plan and put on for the
Unit Project Big Event. Which trick did you like best? Explain why.

____

____

____

____

In what way did that trick illustrate how matter changes?

____

____

____

____

Which trick do you think best fulfilled the ideal of being both
entertaining and instructive? Explain your answer.

____

____

____

____

Describe the trick that was the most fun for the audience.

____

____

____

____

CONTINUITY OF LIFE

Name____ Date__________

In Unit D you'll learn about the reproduction of organisms, the inheritance of traits, and how life has changed through time. For the Unit Project Big Event, you'll prepare and take part in a debate about whether and how to save species of organisms from extinction. Can you list any plants and animals that are in danger of becoming extinct?

What do you think are the main causes for species being in danger of becoming extinct?

____

____

____

____

Does it make any difference to human beings whether microscopic or other small organisms become extinct? Explain your answer.

____

____

____

____

What kinds of species would you work to save if you found out that they were in danger of becoming extinct? Explain why.

____

____

____

____

____

Name_______________________________________ Date___________

UNIT PREVIEW

Consider what you already know about how plants and animals reproduce, how traits are inherited, and how and why species become extinct. What else would you like to learn about these topics? Make a list of your ideas on the lines below.

CHAPTER PREVIEW

Name _________________________________ Date __________

REPRODUCTION

· ·

How are new generations of birds brought into being? In this forest
scene, draw the life cycle of a family of birds.

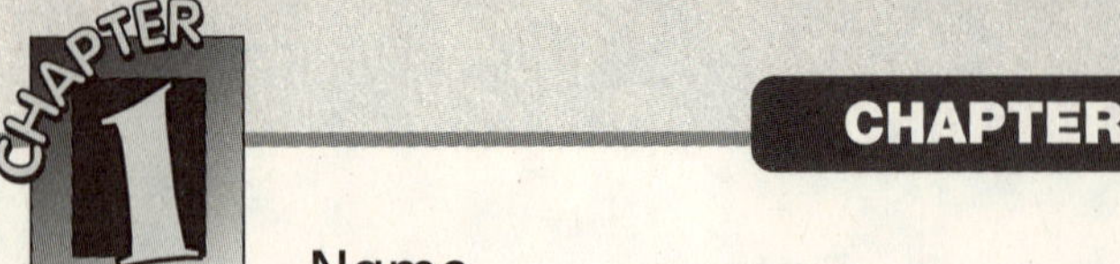

Name ________________________________ Date __________

Dear Journal,

The way that single-celled organisms reproduce is by . . .

____

____

____

____

____

New plants can grow from old plants in these situations . . .

____

____

____

____

____

I think chromosomes are . . .

____

____

____

____

____

If there are two parents of a new organism instead of just one, the new
organism won't have too many chromosomes because . . .

____

____

____

____

____

ACTIVITY RECORD

CHAPTER 1

Name _________________________________ Date __________

DIVIDE AND CONQUER!

Procedure

Write a description of a paramecium you see under the microscope.

____

____

____

____

Make a drawing in the space below of a paramecium you see under the microscope.

Write a description of one specimen on the second slide you study closely.

____

____

____

____

Make a drawing of the specimen on the second slide you have studied closely.

Name ____________________________ Date __________

Record your comparisons of what you saw on the slides with the parameciums on page D7.

____

____

____

____

Record your hypothesis of what accounts for the differences between the first and second slides.

____

____

____

____

Analyze and Conclude

Write the answers to the questions in your book on the lines below.

1. ____

____

2. ____

____

____

3. ____

____

____

4. ____

____

INVESTIGATE FURTHER

Name _______________________________ Date __________

Describe what you found about how other protists reproduce.

Draw how one protist you researched reproduces.

Record the names of the sources you used in your research.

Name _____________________________ Date _________

THE "BUDDING" SYSTEM

Procedure

Write a description of the yeast cells you see under the microscope at low power.

____

____

____

____

____

Make a drawing of what you see when you observe the yeast cells at low power.

Write your inference about what is happening to a cell that seems to have a smaller cell attached to it.

____

____

____

Write a description of what you see when you observe the slide of a hydra.

____

____

____

____

CHAPTER 1

Name ____ Date _____________

Make a drawing of what you see on the slide of a hydra.

Analyze and Conclude

Write the answers to the questions in your book on the lines below.

1. ____

____

2. ____

____

____

3. ____

____

____

4. ____

____

____

5. ____

____

____

Name _______________________ Date _______

Describe some uses of yeast in industry.

Describe how scientists prepare and store yeasts for such uses.

Record the names of the sources you used in your research.

INVESTIGATE FURTHER!

RESEARCH

Page D9

Who was George Washington Carver and when and where did he live?

INVESTIGATE FURTHER!

RESEARCH

Page D17

Describe Carver's ideas on grafting and vegetative propagation.

Record the names of the sources you used in your research.

Name _______________________________________ Date ___________

INVESTIGATION 1

1. What are the advantages of asexual reproduction? What benefits are there to species that reproduce in this way?

____

____

____

____

2. Why might a gardener choose to use vegetative propagation rather than planting a garden with seeds?

____

____

____

____

____

Make a flow chart that shows the basic steps in the fission of an amoeba.

Name _________________________________ Date __________

Splitting Pairs

Procedure

Make a drawing in the space below of two large circles and four small circles. (Make your drawing similar to the one on page D19, but draw the two sets of three side by side instead of one above the other. Label the circles with the same terms used on page D19, though for the two large circles you should write the labels outside of the boundaries of the circles.) **Draw** the chromosomes that should be contained in the immature female sex cell and the immature male sex cell. **Draw** the chromosomes that should be contained in each of the two egg cells. **Draw** the chromosomes that should be contained in each of the two sperm cells.

ACTIVITY RECORD

Name _________________________________ Date ___________

Analyze and Conclude

Write the answers to the questions in your book on the lines below.

1. ____
____
____

2. ____
____

3. ____
____

4. ____

5. ____
____
____

6. ____
____
____

Name _______________________________________ Date __________

Record the animal you researched and the number of chromosomes contained in its sex cells.

Record the names of the sources you used for your research.

ACTIVITY RECORD

CHAPTER 1

Name _________________________________ Date _________

COMBINING CELLS

Procedure

Write your prediction of what will happen to the number of chromosomes when an egg cell and a sperm cell combine.

____

____

____

On the drawing you made on page 194, **draw** a large circle in the middle, beneath the egg cells and the sperm cells. Label this circle. Your drawing should now look like the one on page D21.

Record the number of yarn chromosomes in the zygote you made on the large sheet of paper.

____

Draw the right number of chromosomes in the zygote circle you made on page 194.

Analyze and Conclude

Write the answers to the questions in your book on the lines below.

1. ____

____

2. ____

3. ____

____

____

____

4. ____

____

____

Name _______________________________ Date __________

Describe how a difference in chromosome number causes Down syndrome.

Record the names of other conditions that result from errors in the copying of chromosomes during meiosis.

Record the names of the sources you used in your research.

UNIT PROJECT LINK

Name_______________________________________ Date__________

UNIT PROJECT LINK

Identify any organisms that are endangered that reproduce asexually.

____

____

____

What advantages could asexual reproduction give to a species?

____

____

____

____

____

What disadvantages could asexual reproduction be for a species?

____

____

____

____

____

Does it matter to human beings whether the kind of organisms that reproduce asexually become extinct? Explain your answer.

____

____

____

____

____

Share this information with your group.

CHAPTER 1

Name _______________________________ Date __________

INVESTIGATION 2

1. Imagine that you are a zoologist who has discovered a new organism, the xanaxana. Describe how it reproduces—sexually or asexually. If it reproduces sexually, does meiosis occur? How many chromosomes does it have? What does its offspring look like?

____

____

____

____

____

____

2. What are the advantages and disadvantages of sexual reproduction?

____

____

____

____

____

Draw the sequence of cells and their chromosomes for the process of meiosis in an organism with 4 chromosomes.

Name _______________________________________ Date _______________

REPRODUCTION
. . . .

What is asexual reproduction?

____

____

____

Describe three forms of asexual reproduction.

____

____

____

____

____

____

What is sexual reproduction?

____

____

____

What is the final product of meiosis?

____

____

____

What is an endangered species?

____

____

____

Name _________________________________ Date __________

Think about what you learned in Chapter 1 when you answer the following questions.

1. What surprised you most as you read "Reproduction"?

____

____

____

____

2. How did reading the chapter change your understanding about something you thought you knew?

____

____

____

____

3. What was the most difficult concept for you to understand as you read the chapter? What could you do to understand it better?

____

____

____

____

4. How did reading about endangered species change your thinking about the world around you?

____

____

____

____

Name _________________________________ Date __________

HEREDITY

What would the offspring of these two parents look like? Draw four different adult dogs whose parents are the two at the top.

CHAPTER PREVIEW

Name _______________________ Date _______

Dear Journal,

These features of mine I think I inherited from my mother's side of the family . . .

____

____

____

____

These features of mine I think I inherited from my father's side of the family . . .

____

____

____

____

____

These parts of my body and personality probably were not inherited; rather, they are probably the result of things that have happened to me . . .

____

____

____

____

I think that physical features can skip a generation—pass from grandparents to grandchildren—in this way . . .

____

____

____

____

The structures in cells that contain the chemical codes we inherit are the . . .

____

Name _______________________________________ Date _____________

WHAT CAN YOU DO?

Procedure

Make a chart in the space below to record the class data concerning traits. Write the traits in the left-hand column and the number of students who have that trait in the right-hand column.

Name ___________________________ Date __________

Analyze and Conclude

Write the answers to the questions in your book on the lines below.

1. ____

____

____

2. ____

____

____

3. ____

____

____

Draw a bar graph that reflects the data you collected
in your random poll of 25 people.

Compare this graph with the one you drew of your class data.

ACTIVITY RECORD

Name _______________________________ Date __________

ENVIRONMENTAL INFLUENCE

Procedure

Record your list of environmental conditions that plants need to grow well.

____

____

____

Record the conditions you choose to test for plants B and C.

____

____

Make a chart in the space below to record your observations as the plants grow. Your chart should be an expanded version of the one on page D33.

Name _______________________________ Date _______________

Write your predictions about how the three plants will grow under the conditions you've given them.

____

____

____

____

Each day for a week, **record your observations** in your chart of how well each plant is growing.

Analyze and Conclude

Write the answers to the questions in your book on the lines below.

1. ____

____

2. ____

____

____

3. ____

____

____

4. ____

____

____

5. ____

____

____

INVESTIGATE FURTHER

Name _________________________ Date _____________

Predict what will happen if you give plants *B* and *C* the same conditions that plant *A* has.

Make a chart on a separate sheet of paper like the one you made for the activity Environmental Influence. Keep this chart in your *Science Notebook*. Then each day for a week record your observations of the growth of your three plants, all of which now have the same conditions.

Record the results of your experiment.

Name _______________________________________ Date __________

INVESTIGATION 1

1. Name two inherited traits that can be influenced by the environment. Explain how these traits might be influenced.

____

____

____

____

____

2. Consider two sisters with the same parents. One becomes a champion long-distance runner, the other a lead dancer in a major ballet company. Explain their similarities and differences in terms of heredity and environment.

____

____

____

____

____

Make a chart in the space below in which you can record the inherited traits and the learned traits you think might be involved in: (1) scoring a soccer goal and (2) playing a violin solo.

Name ___________________________ Date ___________

SCRAMBLED GENES

Procedure

Make a chart in the space below to record your data. Your chart should be an expanded version of the one on page D39. The chart should be big enough to record four disk colors. **Record** in this chart the data you obtain when you empty the *female* cup into the *egg cell* and the *male* cup into the *sperm cell*.

Record your prediction of what the combination of genes would be if you did steps 6 and 7 again.

____

____

____

____

Make charts in the space below and on the next page for five more trials. Each time, record the data you obtain when you empty the cups into the cells. If you run out of space to make charts, use a separate sheet of paper and then keep that sheet in your *Science Notebook*.

Name _______________________________________ Date ___________

Analyze and Conclude

Write the answers to the questions in your book on the lines below.

1. ____
____
____
____

2. ____
____
____

Name____ Date__________

UNIT PROJECT LINK

Identify some endangered plants or animals that are "specialists."

____

____

____

____

Describe why each of the plants and animals you identified is considered a specialist.

____

____

____

____

____

____

Are specialists more likely to be endangered than generalists?
Explain your answer.

____

____

____

____

Describe how you could organize your data about these endangered
species into a poster or large chart.

____

____

____

____

Share this information with your group.

Name _______________________________ Date __________

INHERITING TRAITS

Procedure

Make a chart in the space below like the one on page D40. In your chart **record the results** you obtain for each of the six times you flip the disk for the sperm cell. **Record the results** you obtain for each of the six times you flip the disk for the egg cell. **Record the combination** of genes in the *Zygote* by combining the results you obtained for each trial.

Name _______________________________________ Date _____________

Analyze and Conclude

Write the answers to the questions in your book on the lines below.

1. ____

____

2. ____

____

____

____

3. ____

____

____

INVESTIGATE FURTHER!

TAKE ACTION

Page D41

Describe some ways that you might be able to help those who are left-handed.

Describe some ways that you might be able to help those who are nearsighted.

Name _______________________________________ Date __________

ALL IN THE FAMILY

Procedure

Record your observations about the ear lobes of each individual in the pedigree chart. In the space below, **make a chart** like the one shown on page D42. For each individual in the chart, write either *free* or *attached,* depending on how you interpret the gene combination for that person.

Name ___________________________________ Date ___________

Analyze and Conclude

Write the answers to the questions in your book on the lines below.

1. ____
____
____
____

2. ____
____
____
____
____
____

3. ____
____
____
____

Name ______________________________________ Date __________

INVESTIGATION 2

1. Distinguish between dominant genes and recessive genes for a trait.

____

____

____

____

____

2. In Mendel's experiments, he crossed tall plants (gene combination TT) with short plants (tt). Use a Punnett square like the one on page D45 to show the possible gene combinations in the offspring. Describe each type.

Imagine that you're the writer of a cookbook—a cookbook of medicines. One of your recipes is for the making of insulin. In the spaces below, write a title for the recipe, the ingredients the cook needs to obtain, and the steps the cook should follow.

Title: ____________________________________

Ingredients: ______________________________

____

Steps: ___________________________________

____

____

____

____

CHAPTER WRAP-UP

Name ____ Date ____________

HEREDITY

What are inherited traits and learned traits?

____

____

____

____

Explain how some inherited traits can be influenced by the environment.
Use an example in your explanation.

____

____

____

____

____

____

How are traits inherited?

____

____

____

____

What is the difference between a dominant trait and a recessive trait?

____

____

____

____

____

Name _________________________________ Date _________

Think about what you learned in Chapter 2 when you answer the following questions.

1. What did you think was the most interesting thing you learned as you read "Heredity"?

____

____

____

____

2. Look again at the questions you answered on page 204. Of the features you listed as being inherited from your mother's or father's side of the family, which do you now think are inherited traits that have not been influenced by the environment?

____

____

____

____

____

3. Which of those features you listed do you now think are inherited traits that have been influenced by the environment?

____

____

____

____

____

4. What is a recessive trait that you think you might have in your genes but is not expressed in you?

____

____

____

____

Name _______________________________ Date ___________

CHANGE THROUGH TIME

The drawing at the bottom of this page shows a scene from the western United States—a rugged country of mountains and not much water. But during the Jurassic Period, that same area was a swampy flatland where dinosaurs ruled. Draw a Jurassic scene in the space below.

Name _________________________________ Date _________

Dear Journal,

I've seen fossils of these organisms . . .

____

____

____

____

Fossils are helpful to scientists because . . .

____

____

____

____

Evidence that evolution of organisms has occurred and is still occurring
includes . . .

____

____

____

____

I think the way that plants and animals evolve over time is . . .

____

____

____

____

Name _______________________________________ Date ____________

EXAMINE A FOSSIL

Procedure

Record your observations of the first fossil you examine.

____

____

____

____

Record your observations of the first fossil using a hand lens.

____

____

____

____

Make a drawing of the fossil that includes all the details you can see,
with labels for the parts you can identify.

Record your observations of the second fossil you examine.

____

____

____

____

ACTIVITY RECORD

Use with pages D52–D53.

Name _______________________ Date _______________

Record your observations of the second fossil using a hand lens.

____

____

____

____

Make a drawing of the second fossil that includes all the details you can see, with labels for the parts you can identify.

Analyze and Conclude

Write the answers to the questions in your book on the lines below.

1. ____

____

2. ____

____

____

3. ____

____

____

4. ____

____

____

____

INVESTIGATE FURTHER

Name _______________________________________ Date _____________

Identify the first fossil you examined and tell what
you learned from and about it.

Identify the second fossil you examined and tell what you
learned about it.

Name ___________________________ Date __________

MAKE A MODEL FOSSIL

Procedure

Write your prediction of what the clay will look like after you remove the shell.

____

____

____

____

Record your observations of the surface of the clay once you have removed the shell. **Make a drawing** of your observations.

____

____

____

Record your observations of the hardened plaster of Paris once you have separated the plaster from the clay. **Make a drawing** of your observations.

____

____

____

ACTIVITY RECORD

CHAPTER
3

Name _______________________________ Date ___________

Analyze and Conclude

Write the answers to the questions in your book on the lines below.

1. ____
____
____

2. ____
____
____
____

3. ____
____
____
____

4. ____
____
____
____

5. ____
____
____
____
____

UNIT PROJECT LINK

Name________________________________ Date__________

UNIT PROJECT LINK

Identify the endangered animal whose footprint you plan to make a fossil of. Give reasons for your choice.

____

____

____

____

Describe the size and shape of the footprint.

____

____

____

____

What method do you plan to use in making this "fossil"? Will it be a mold or a cast?

____

____

____

____

List the materials you will need to make your "fossil."

____

____

____

____

Share this information with your group.

Name ____ Date ___________

INVESTIGATION 1

1. Describe two ways by which fossils can form.

____

____

____

____

____

2. The petrified remains of complete skeletons of animals are rare. Why do you think this is so?

____

____

____

____

Make an outline in the space below of the geologic eras and their periods. Beside each name write how many million years ago the time was.

Name _______________________________ Date __________

OUT ON A LIMB

Procedure

Record your observations of the ways in which the front limbs of the four animals are similar.

____

____

____

____

____

____

Record your observations of the ways in which the front limbs of the four animals are different.

____

____

____

____

____

Record your comparisons of the models of the limb-bone structures of the four animals.

____

____

____

____

____

____

____

ACTIVITY RECORD

CHAPTER 3

Name ___________________________ Date ___________

Analyze and Conclude

Write the answers to the questions in your book on the lines below.

1. ____
____
____
____

2. ____
____
____
____

3. ____
____
____
____

4. ____
____
____
____

5. ____
____
____
____

Name ___________________________________ Date ___________

Identify the animal whose front limb is most like a human being's.

Support your identification with evidence.

Identify the animal whose front limb is most different from a human being's. Support your identification with evidence.

Infer the reason why the one set of bones is so much like our own and the other set is so different.

Name _________________________________ Date ___________

INVESTIGATION 2

1. How do structural similarities among living things support the idea that living things are related?

____

____

____

____

____

2. What characteristics do you think early breeders found in the wolf that they bred into the domesticated dog?

____

____

____

____

Imagine that you're Charles Darwin on the 1831 voyage of the *Beagle* around the world. You've been on the Galapagos Islands for a few days now and have made some important observations about finches. As Charles Darwin, write an entry in your ship's log telling what you've seen that seems significant. (You'll continue this entry later in the chapter.)

Darwin's Log

____

____

____

____

____

____

____

____

Name __________________________________ Date __________

A VARIETY OF PEANUTS

Procedure

Record your measurements of the longest peanut and the shortest
peanut you find.

____

Record the difference in length between the longest and shortest peanut.

____

Make a graph on graph paper on which you can record the length of
peanuts. Keep this graph in your *Science Notebook*. On the horizontal
axis, number the squares for recording the lengths of as many peanuts as
you have. **Record the length** of the longest peanut above the first number. **Record the length** of the shortest peanut above the last number.

____

Write your prediction of the length of peanut that you will measure
most often.

____

____

Record the length of each peanut on your graph.

Analyze and Conclude

Write the answers to the questions in your book on the lines below.

1. ____

____

____

____

2. ____

____

____

____

ACTIVITY RECORD

CHAPTER 3

Name _______________________________ Date __________

3. ____
____
____
____

4. ____
____
____
____

Hypothesize about whether you will find any correlation between peanut length and peanut mass.

Record the results of your experiment: What was the greatest mass, the least mass, and the most common mass among the peanuts?

Did your hypothesis match your results? Explain your answer.

Name _______________________________________ Date ___________

INVESTIGATION 3

1. How did Darwin's theory of natural selection explain how varieties of species came to be?

____

____

____

____

____

____

2. How was the work of Mendel influential in explaining Darwin's theory?

____

____

____

____

____

____

You're Darwin again, back on the *Beagle* and fresh from your observations on the Galápagos Islands. Continue your log entry. Write what you infer from your observations of the 13 varieties of finches.

Darwin's Log

____

____

____

____

____

____

Name ____ Date __________

CHANGE THROUGH TIME

What do fossils tell us about life—past and present?

____

____

____

____

What is the difference between a mold fossil and a cast fossil?

____

____

____

____

What evidence do scientists have that evolution occurs?

____

____

____

____

How does the process of natural selection affect species?

____

____

____

____

What is a mutation and how can it be beneficial?

____

____

____

____

Name _________________________________ Date ____________

Think about what you learned in Chapter 3 when you answer the following questions.

1. What did you learn in reading "Change Through Time" that makes you think differently about a pet you have or have had?

____

____

____

____

2. What was the most interesting thing you learned as you read the chapter?

____

____

____

____

3. Describe something you learned that might interest someone else in your family.

____

____

____

____

4. Have you been convinced by reading the chapter that human beings evolved from other species over time? Explain why or why not.

____

____

____

____

UNIT WRAP-UP

Name____ Date__________

UNIT PROJECT WRAP-UP

Think about the Unit Project Big Event, the debate about saving
endangered species. Which side were you on, and which argument
did you make in the debate?

____

____

____

____

____

What do you think was the most persuasive argument made for saving an endangered species?

____

____

____

____

____

What do you think was the most persuasive argument made against
saving an endangered species?

____

____

____

____

____

Describe the most impressive fossil made for the display.

____

____

____

____

UNIT E

Name_________________________________ Date__________

OCEANOGRAPHY

In Unit E you'll learn about ocean water, ocean organisms, the ocean floor, and ocean currents and waves. For the Unit Project Big Event, you'll help create an undersea nature lodge, where your knowledge of oceanography will be displayed across a picture window. Describe the picture you think of when you think of the ocean.

____

____

____

____

If you could make a movie to teach people about ocean life and the environment in which these organisms live, what scenes would you use to capture the viewers' interest at the beginning?

____

____

____

____

How could you explain the characteristics of ocean water and its movements in this movie—or a moving picture you create?

____

____

____

____

What would it be like to take a vacation at an underwater resort? Write a description of such a vacation. You may want to use drawings to make your description clear.

____

____

____

____

Name_______________________________ Date__________

UNIT PREVIEW

There are probably many things you already know about Earth's oceans. What are some other things you'd like to learn? Make a list of your ideas on the lines below.

____

____

____

____

____

____

____

____

____

____

____

____

____

____

____

Name _________________________________ Date __________

OCEAN WATER

This is the ocean floor not far from shore. Can you see any living things?
Color in the ones you find, and add others you can think of.

Name _________________________________ Date __________

Dear Journal,

This is how ocean water feels, tastes, and smells . . .

____

____

____

____

____

I think the salt in saltwater is the result of . . .

____

____

____

____

____

____

People can float better in ocean water than in fresh water because . . .

____

____

____

These are ten types of living things that can only live in ocean water . . .

____

____

____

____

ACTIVITY RECORD

Name _______________________________________ Date ____________

A Closer Look at Ocean Water

Procedure

Record your observations of the sample of ocean water in the clear container.

____

____

____

Record your observations of the drop of ocean water on the slide under the microscope.

____

____

____

Write your prediction of what you will see when the water evaporates.

____

____

____

Record your observations as the water evaporates.

____

____

____

Record your observations with a hand lens of any material left behind in the container when evaporation is complete.

____

____

Record your observations of what happens when you add tap water to the container.

____

____

Name _______________________________________ Date _________

Analyze and Conclude

Write the answers to the questions in your book on the lines below.

1. ____

____

2. ____

____

3. ____

____

____

Predict how your observations would differ if you were using fresh water in the activity instead of ocean water.

Record your observations of what happens when you repeat the activity using fresh water instead of ocean water.

Infer from your data the difference between ocean water and fresh water.

INVESTIGATION CLOSE

Name _________________________________ Date _________

INVESTIGATION 1

1. What kinds of materials are found in ocean water?

____

____

____

____

2. You are given two samples of water and told that one is ocean water and one is water from a lake. Without tasting them, how might you determine which is which?

____

____

____

____

Make a flow chart in the space below that explains the process by which ocean water becomes so salty. Begin with rain falling on land.

Name _____________________________________ Date __________

LIGHTING THE WATER

Procedure

Make a chart in the space below to record your observations of the Secchi disk. Your chart should be an expanded version of the one on page E12. How many entries you make will depend on how deep your bucket or can is. **Record** in your chart how well you can see the disk in the water at a depth of 10 cm and then every 10 cm deeper.

Record your measurement of the depth below the flour water's surface at which you can no longer see the disk.

____

Write your prediction of the depth to which you would be able to see the disk if you added 100 g of flour to the water.

____

Record your measurement of the depth below the flour water's surface at which you can no longer see the disk after adding 100 g of flour to the water.

____

ACTIVITY RECORD

CHAPTER 1

Name _______________________________________ Date __________

Analyze and Conclude

Write the answers to the questions in your book on the lines below.

1. ____

   ____

2. ____

   ____

3. ____

   ____

4. ____

   ____

   ____

INVESTIGATE FURTHER!

RESEARCH

Page E13

Describe the role that light plays in determining the color of ocean water.

Describe how the amount of life in the water affects its color at different places.

Record the names of the sources you used in your research.

Name _______________________________________ Date ____________

DENSE WATER

Procedure

Make a chart in the space below like the one on page E14.

Record in your chart the temperature of the warm water, and then **record the length** of the straw that is under water.

Record in your chart the temperature of the cold water.

Write your prediction of how much of the straw will be under water in cold water.

____

____

____

Record in your chart the length of the straw that is under water in cold water.

ACTIVITY RECORD

Name _________________________________ Date __________

Write your prediction of how much of the straw will be under water in salt water.

____

____

____

Record in your chart the length of the straw that is under water in salt water.

Analyze and Conclude

Write the answers to the questions in your book on the lines below.

1. ____

____

____

2. ____

____

____

____

____

____

Use with page E16.

Name ___________________________________ Date ___________

UNDER PRESSURE

Procedure

Record your measurement of how far the water squirts out of the carton when it is filled to the 5-cm mark.

____

Record your measurement of how far the water squirts out of the carton when it is filled to the 10-cm mark.

____

Write your prediction of how far the water will squirt out of the carton when it is filled to the 15-cm mark.

____

Record your measurement of how far the water squirts out of the carton when it is filled to the 15-cm mark.

____

Write your prediction of how far the water will squirt out of the carton when it is filled to the 20-cm mark.

____

Record your measurement of how far the water squirts out of the carton when it is filled to the 20-cm mark.

____

Analyze and Conclude

Write the answers to the questions in your book on the lines below.

1. ____

____

____

2. ____

____

3. ____

____

INVESTIGATE FURTHER

Name _______________________________________ Date ___________

Describe what and where the Dead Sea is.

Draw a map of the Dead Sea in the space below.

Infer whether its water is more or less dense than ocean water.
Give reasons for your inference.

Record the names of the sources you used in your research.

Name ____ Date _______________

INVESTIGATE FURTHER!

EXPERIMENT

Page E21

Predict how the results of the activity on page E16 would vary if you punched holes at 2 cm, 6 cm, and 10 cm.

Describe the results of your experiment and explain the reasons for what you observed.

Name _________________________________ Date __________

INVESTIGATION 2

1. What are the physical properties of ocean water?

____

____

____

2. What do you think would happen to any organisms found at the bottom of the Marianas Trench if they were brought suddenly to the surface? Explain your answer.

____

____

____

Each of the pairs below are equal in volume but have different characteristics. For each pair, tell which is denser and explain your reasoning.

Ocean water or fresh water?

____

____

____

Warm water or cold water?

____

____

____

Ocean water at the surface or ocean water at a depth of 100 m?

____

____

____

Water at a temperature of 5°C or water at a temperature of 1°C?

____

____

Name _______________________________________ Date __________

LET THE SUN SHINE

Procedure

Record your observations of the setup containing the *Elodea* after 10 minutes.

____

____

____

____

Write your prediction of any changes that will occur over 24 hours.

____

____

____

____

Record your observations of the setup containing the *Elodea* after 24 hours.

____

____

____

____

Analyze and Conclude

Write the answers to the questions in your book on the lines below.

1. ____

____

____

2. ____

____

____

UNIT PROJECT LINK

Name_______________________________ Date__________

UNIT PROJECT LINK
. . . .

What are some ocean organisms that you know something about
and would especially like to do more research on?

____

____

____

What organisms do you think it would be important to include in
your moving picture so that you make a balanced presentation of
ocean life?

____

____

____

What features of these organisms should be investigated?

____

____

____

Where could you find pictures of ocean organisms?

____

____

Write a brief story you think would be good to use in your moving
picture. This story would be the way you could organize your
research findings so you could make an interesting presentation.

____

____

____

____

____

Share this information with your group.

Name _______________________________________ Date _____________

INVESTIGATION 3

1. What organisms might you find as part of the plankton, nekton, and benthos groups?

____

____

____

____

2. Why do you think most plantlike organisms are found in ocean water no deeper than about 9 or 10 m?

____

____

Make a labeled drawing in the space below that illustrates where the three groups of organisms live in the ocean. Include the name of the groups in your drawing as well as sketches of specific examples.

CHAPTER WRAP-UP

Name ____ Date ____________

OCEAN WATER
· ·

What makes up ocean water?

____

____

____

Why is the salinity of ocean water greater than that of fresh water?

____

____

____

____

____

What are the properties of ocean water?

____

____

____

How does water temperature, density, and pressure change from the
ocean surface to the ocean bottom?

____

____

____

____

Describe the three groups of living things in ocean water.

____

____

____

Name _______________________________ Date ___________

Think about what you learned in Chapter 1 when you answer the following questions.

1. What did you find most interesting as you read about ocean water?

____

____

____

____

____

2. What did you learn in the chapter that you might like to describe to an adult in your family or your neighborhood?

____

____

____

____

____

3. What did you learn that changed something you thought you knew about the ocean and its life?

____

____

____

____

____

4. What else would you like to learn about ocean life? How could you go about learning more?

____

____

____

____

____

Name ____ Date ______________

THE OCEAN FLOOR

You've learned about benthos, organisms that live on the ocean floor.
What is their environment like? Draw what you think the ocean floor
looks like beneath the deep ocean.

Name _______________________ Date _____________

Dear Journal,

I think the ocean floor near shore looks like . . .

____

____

____

____

____

These features of the deep ocean floor are similar to natural features on land . . .

____

____

____

____

____

Scientists map the ocean floor by . . .

____

____

____

____

____

This is what I know about underwater vehicles . . .

____

____

____

____

____

ACTIVITY RECORD

CHAPTER
2

Name _______________________________ Date ____________

GRAPHING THE OCEAN FLOOR

Procedure

Make a graph below or on a separate sheet of graph paper of the data in the table on page E30. Keep this graph in your *Science Notebook*.

Analyze and Conclude

Write the answers to the questions in your book on the lines below.

1. ____
____
____

2. ____
____

3. ____
____
____
____

Name _________________________________ Date _________

MODELING OCEAN SEDIMENTS

Procedure

Record your observations of the two bottles several minutes after pouring clay into one and the mixed sediments into the other.

____

____

____

Make sketches of the two bottles after having observed them for several minutes.

Record your observations of the two bottles 1 hour after pouring powdered clay into one and mixed sediments into the other.

____

____

____

Make sketches of the two bottles after having observed them for 1 hour.

ACTIVITY RECORD

Name ________________________________ Date __________

Analyze and Conclude

Write the answers to the questions in your book on the lines below.

1. ____
____
____
____
____

2. ____
____
____

INVESTIGATE FURTHER!

RESEARCH

Page E39

Describe how water on land deposits sediments that look very similar to those deposited in the ocean.

What are those sediments called once they harden?

Record the names of the sources you used in your research.

Name _______________________________________ Date ____________

INVESTIGATION 1

1. Draw and describe the features of the ocean floor.

2. Why is looking at the sedimentary layers of the ocean floor like looking at a time line?

____

____

____

____

Make two lists in the space below: (1) sources of inorganic sediments and (2) sources of organic sediments.

Name _________________________________ Date ___________

HEAR THE DISTANCE

Procedure

Record how long it takes to do 20 timed claps.

____

Make your calculation of the time it takes the sound of one clap to travel from you to the wall and back again.

Record your measurement of the distance between your location and the wall.

____

Make your calculation of the speed of sound in the space below.

Write your method for how to use sound to determine distance.

____

____

____

____

____

ACTIVITY RECORD

Name _______________________________________ Date _____________

Record your data in the space below each time you use your method to find different distances from the wall.

Analyze and Conclude

Write the answers to the questions in your book on the lines below.

1. ____

____

2. ____

____

____

____

3. ____

____

____

____

Name_______________________________ Date__________

UNIT PROJECT LINK

At what depth and how far from land would you locate the site of
your undersea lodge? Give reasons for your answer.

____

____

____

After looking at a map, identify some locations that might be pos-
sibilities for your undersea lodge.

____

____

____

____

Identify safety factors that you would have to take into account.

____

____

____

____

Draw illustrations in the space below to show the topography that
visitors to the lodge would see.

Share this information with your group.

Use with page E42.

Name _________________________________ Date __________

MODELING SONAR

Procedure

Record the measurement of the time it takes the wave motion to travel to the doorknob and back to your hand.

____

Record the measurement of the distance from your hand to the door-knob.

____

Record the measurements of time as you and your partner repeat step 2 five more times.

1. ____

2. ____

3. ____

4. ____

5. ____

Make your calculation of the average time for the wave motion to travel to the doorknob and back to your hand.

Make a drawing in the space below that shows the action of the wave, the distance to and from your hand to the door, and the average time a wave takes to complete the journey.

ACTIVITY RECORD

Name ____ Date _____________

Make your calculation of the rate of travel of the wave.

Analyze and Conclude

Write the answers to the questions in your book on the lines below.

1. ____

____

____

____

Use the space below to make your calculation.

2.

Name _____________________________ Date _________

INVESTIGATION 2

1. Describe some methods that have been used to explore the ocean floor.

____

____

____

____

____

2. Using sonar, a scientist aboard a ship notes that for the first five pulses the signal takes longer to return each time. For the next five pulses the signal returns faster each time. What is the ship passing over?

____

____

____

Imagine you were aboard the HMS *Challenger* in 1872 when it sailed thousands of kilometers to measure ocean depths and collect deep-sea samples. Your job is to write a report to the Royal Society of London, which provided the funds for the expedition. Tell the royalty back in London about what you are doing and what some of your discoveries have been.

Name _________________________________ Date _____________

THE OCEAN FLOOR

What are the features of the ocean floor? Write a brief description of each feature.

____

____

____

____

____

____

____

____

____

What are the two types of sediments on the ocean floor?

____

____

How do scientists study the ocean floor?

____

____

____

Describe how sonar mapping is accomplished.

____

____

____

____

Name _______________________________________ Date ____________

Think about what you learned in Chapter 2 when you answer the following questions.

1. What surprised you most about the ocean floor?

____

____

____

____

2. What did you find most interesting as you read the chapter?

____

____

____

____

3. If you could visit one place on the ocean floor, what would it be? Explain.

____

____

____

____

4. What did you find most difficult to understand in the chapter? What could you do to understand it better?

____

____

____

____

Name _______________________________ Date __________

MOVING OCEAN WATER

How does ocean water move? Complete this picture of an ocean coastline by showing how the ocean moves.

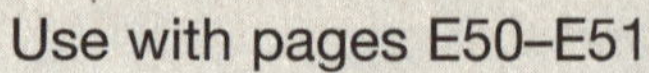

Name _________________________________ Date _____________

Dear Journal,

I believe ocean currents are caused by . . .

____

____

____

Ships use ocean currents to . . .

____

____

____

Waves can be described by these characteristics . . .

____

____

____

Ocean waves are caused by . . .

____

____

____

Tides are . . .

____

____

____

I think tides are caused by . . .

____

____

____

Name _________________________________ Date _________

CURRENT TRENDS

Procedure

Write your prediction of what will happen if you gently blow across the
surface of the water through a straw.

____

____

____

Record your observations of what happens when you gently blow across
the surface of the water through a straw.

____

____

____

Make a sketch of what you observe when you gently blow across the surface of the water through a straw.

Write your prediction of what will happen if you blow harder across the
surface of the water.

____

____

____

Name _________________________________ Date _________

Record your observations of what happens when you blow harder across the surface of the water.

____

____

____

Make a sketch of what you observe when you blow harder across the surface of the water.

Analyze and Conclude

Write the answers to the questions in your book on the lines below.

1. ____

____

____

2. ____

____

____

3. ____

____

____

____

INVESTIGATE FURTHER

Name ________________________________ Date ____________

Describe the location of the Sargasso Sea.

Record your findings about currents in this sea.

Record the names of the sources you used in your research.

Name ______________________________ Date __________

MODELING DENSITY CURRENTS

Procedure

Write your prediction of what will happen when you pour the contents of the cup into the jar.

____

____

Record your observations of what you observe 2 minutes after pouring the contents of the cup into the jar.

____

____

Write your prediction of how the liquid will change in 10 minutes.

____

____

Record your observations of what you observe after letting the jar of liquid sit for 10 minutes.

____

____

____

Analyze and Conclude

Write the answers to the questions in your book on the lines below.

1. ____

____

2. ____

____

3. ____

____

UNIT
E

Name_______________________________________ Date__________

UNIT PROJECT LINK

Describe where you and your group have decided to locate your
undersea lodge.

____

____

____

What kind of deep-sea vehicle could you use for one-day side trips?

____

____

____

What features of the ocean floor or ocean organisms do you think
it would be most important for the visitors to see?

____

____

____

____

Describe a one-day side trip visitors will be able to take at your
undersea lodge. How does it relate to the world's ocean currents?
What will the visitors see?

____

____

____

____

____

Share this information with your group.

Name _______________________________________ Date ___________

INVESTIGATION 1

1. What role does wind play in creating currents?

____

____

____

2. How are surface currents and deep currents alike? How are they different?

____

____

____

____

____

____

Make a flow chart that shows how a raindrop that falls on Greece (a country on the north shore of the Mediterranean Sea) ends up at the bottom of the Atlantic Ocean.

Name _________________________________ Date __________

MAKING WAVES

Procedure

Record your observations of what happens when you blow gently down the side of the cardboard.

____

____

Write your prediction of what will happen if you blow harder down the side of the cardboard.

____

____

Record your observations of what happens when you blow harder down the side of the cardboard.

____

____

Write your prediction of what will happen if you blow on the water a longer period of time.

____

____

Record your observations of what happens when you blow on the water for a longer period of time.

____

____

Analyze and Conclude

Write the answers to the questions in your book on the lines below.

1. ____

____

____

Name _______________________________ Date _________

2. ____

____

____

3. ____

____

____

4. ____

____

Predict how an island might affect the size of waves.
Give reasons for your prediction.

Describe the results of your experiment.

Infer how you think the island would be affected over time.

Name _________________________________ Date ___________

WAVE MOTION

Procedure

Make a chart in the space below like the one on page E64. Each time
you make a wave, **record** in this chart the height of the wave and your
observations of the ribbon.

Make sketches in the space below to show what you observe as you
make your waves.

Name _______________________________ Date __________

Analyze and Conclude

Write the answers to the questions in your book on the lines below.

1. ____

____

2. ____

____

3. ____

____

Describe what a tsunami is and what causes one.

Describe where tsunamis are most likely to occur.

What damage can a tsunami do?

How are people warned about tsunamis?

Record the names of the sources you used in your research.

Name _______________________________ Date __________

INVESTIGATION 2

1. How are waves formed?

____

____

____

2. Would you expect larger waves to form from a wind with a fetch of 1 km or 3 km? Explain your answer.

____

____

____

List the factors that determine the size of a wave.

____

____

____

Draw a series of ocean waves in the space below, with labels for all the parts you know.

Name ____ Date ______________

MAKING A TIDE MODEL

Procedure

Record your inference on which of the two numbered sides of Earth the ocean is deepest when the Moon is located nearest to side 1.

____

____

Make a sketch in the space below of your model when the Moon is located nearest to side 1.

Record your inference on which of the two numbered sides of Earth the ocean is deepest after you have modeled the passing of 6 hours in Earth's rotation.

____

____

Make a sketch in the space below of your model 6 hours later in Earth's rotation.

Name _______________________________ Date _____________

Analyze and Conclude

Write the answers to the questions in your book on the lines below.

1. ____

   ____

2. ____

   ____

3. ____

4. ____

   ____

   ____

Sketch the positions of the Sun, Moon, and Earth when they are in a line.

Infer what the effect will be on Earth's oceans when the Sun is in this position.

Name ________________________________ Date ___________

INVESTIGATION 3

1. Use a sketch to show how the Moon's gravity causes tides on Earth.

2. How many low tides do most shore areas on Earth have during two days and two nights? Explain your answer.

____

____

____

____

Make two drawings in the space below. Show the positions of Earth, the Moon, and the Sun at (1) spring tide and (2) neap tide.

CHAPTER WRAP-UP

Name _____________________________ Date __________

MOVING OCEAN WATER

What determines the speed and direction of ocean surface currents?

____

____

____

What causes deep ocean currents?

____

____

____

What is the Gulf Stream?

____

____

____

____

What causes ocean waves?

____

____

What are the three factors that determine how large ocean waves are?

____

____

____

What are tides and what causes them?

____

____

____

____

Name _______________________________________ Date ___________

Think about what you learned in Chapter 3 when you answer the following questions.

1. What did you learn as you read "Moving Ocean Water" that surprised you most?

____

____

____

____

2. What was the most difficult concept to understand as you read about ocean currents?

____

____

____

____

____

3. What did you learn about tides that explains something you always wondered about?

____

____

____

____

____

4. What did you learn that you think someone in your family might be interested in learning?

____

____

____

____

Name _______________________________   Date ___________

OCEAN RESOURCES

Oil spill! Show how the beach, birds, and sea creatures might be affected
if an oil tanker broke apart offshore.

CHAPTER PREVIEW

Name _________________________ Date _________

Dear Journal,

These are the kinds of seafood I like . . .

____

____

____

____

The reason we don't get drinking water directly from the ocean is . . .

____

____

____

We get these resources from the sea . . .

____

____

____

____

____

An oil spill in the ocean can result in these problems . . .

____

____

____

____

____

Other things that can pollute the ocean include . . .

____

____

____

____

____

CHAPTER 4

Name ____________________________ Date __________

WHAT YOU SEE FROM THE SEA

Procedure

Make a list of everything you can see in the classroom, the school, and your home that comes from the sea.

____

____

____

____

____

____

____

Analyze and Conclude

Write the answers to the questions in your book on the lines below.

1. ____________________________________

____

____

____

2. ____________________________________

____

____

Name _________________________________ Date __________

DESALINATION

Procedure

Record your observations of any changes you see in the setup when you shut the lamp off after 30 minutes.

____

____

____

Write a description of a process though which you could transform ocean water into drinkable water. You will have to think of a way to get the salt out of the ocean water or make pure water by using ocean water as a raw material.

____

____

____

____

____

____

Make a drawing in the space below of the process you have described to transform ocean water into drinkable water.

Name _________________________________ Date __________

Analyze and Conclude

Write the answers to the questions in your book on the lines below.

1. ____

____

____

2. ____

____

____

____

____

Name _______________________________________ Date ___________

OBTAINING ENERGY

Procedure

Make a list of as many forms of energy as you can. For each form of energy you list, write the raw materials needed and describe the equipment used to change those raw materials into usable forms.

____

____

____

____

____

Write your hypothesis about what untapped forms of energy there might be in the ocean.

____

____

____

____

Make a sketch in the space below of the model or poster you are making about one energy-source idea.

ACTIVITY RECORD

CHAPTER
4

Name _______________________________ Date ___________

Write a description of how you would present your model or poster to the class. Tell what you would say in your presentation.

____
____
____
____
____
____
____
____
____
____

Analyze and Conclude

Write the answers to the questions in your book on the lines below.

1. ____
____
____
____
____

2. ____
____
____
____
____

Name_______________________________ Date__________

UNIT PROJECT LINK

Describe the sea life that thrives near the site of your undersea lodge.

____

____

____

____

____

Which of those organisms could provide ocean farming products? Give reasons for your choices.

____

____

____

Where might be good places near your lodge for an ocean farm?

____

____

____

Make a diagram of an idea you have for aquatic technology.

Share this information with your group.

Name ___________________________ Date ___________

INVESTIGATION 1

1. Name six resources that come from the oceans.

____

____

____

2. Would tidal energy be a good source of energy for the town you live in? Why or why not?

____

____

____

____

On the lines below, write a letter to a government official. You can take the role of an environmentalist, giving reasons why the government should restrict fishing in ocean waters offshore. Or, you can take the role of the owner of a seafood company, telling the official why fishing in ocean waters is important to society.

____

____

____

____

____

____

____

____

____

____

____

Name _______________________________ Date _______________

INVESTIGATING OIL SPILLS

Procedure

Write your prediction of what will happen if you place a small drop of oil in the water.

____

____

Record your observations of what happens when you place a small drop of oil in the water.

____

____

Record your observations of how the oil and water interact after you have shaken the container of water and oil.

____

____

Record your observations of a feather observed with a hand lens.

____

____

____

Record your observations of the feather observed with a hand lens after you have soaked it in water and then blotted it dry with a paper towel.

____

____

____

Record your observations of the feather observed with a hand lens after you have soaked it in oil and blotted it dry with a paper towel.

____

____

____

ACTIVITY RECORD

CHAPTER 4

Name _______________________________ Date __________

Analyze and Conclude

Write the answers to the questions in your book on the lines below.

1. ____
____
____

2. ____
____
____

3. ____
____
____

Predict the effect an oil spill might have on bird eggs in nests along the coast.

Describe the results of your experiment on a hard-boiled egg.

Infer from your results how an oil spill might affect bird eggs in nests along the coast.

Name _____________________________ Date __________

CLEANING UP THE MESS

Procedure

Record your hypothesis of what method you could use to clean up the oil in your model oil spill.

____

____

____

Write a description of the cleanup method you will try.

____

____

____

Record how effective your method was in cleaning up the oil.

____

____

____

Record your hypothesis of another method you could use to clean up the oil in your model oil spill.

____

____

____

Write a description of the cleanup method you will try.

____

____

____

Report how effective your second method was in cleaning up the oil.

____

____

____

Name _________________________________ Date _____________

Record your hypothesis of a third method you could use to clean up the oil in your model oil spill.

____

____

____

Write a description of the cleanup method you will try.

____

____

____

Record how effective your third method was in cleaning up the oil.

____

____

____

Analyze and Conclude

Write the answers to the questions in your book on the lines below.

1. ____

____

____

2. ____

____

____

____

3. ____

____

____

Name _______________________________ Date __________

INVESTIGATION 2

1. Name three kinds of pollution that affect the oceans.

____

____

____

2. Describe why you do or do not think ocean pollution threatens the quality of all life on Earth.

____

____

____

____

____

Make a flow chart in the space below that shows how chemicals used on a farm could harm a person who eats ocean fish for dinner.

CHAPTER WRAP-UP

Name _________________________________ Date _____________

OCEAN RESOURCES

What resources can the oceans provide?

____

____

____

____

____

____

What is pollution?

____

____

____

What kinds of materials can pollute the oceans?

____

____

____

____

How does pollution affect the oceans and their resources?

____

____

____

____

____

____

Name ____ Date ____________

Think about what you learned in Chapter 4 when you answer the following questions.

1. What did you learn as you read "Ocean Resources" that most affected your understanding of the ocean?

____

____

____

____

2. What was the most interesting thing you learned about the resources that the ocean holds?

____

____

____

____

3. What did you learn about ocean pollution that might make you reconsider something in your own life?

____

____

____

____

4. What else would you like to learn about ocean resources? What could you do to find out?

____

____

____

____

Name_____________________________________ Date__________

UNIT PROJECT WRAP-UP

Think about the Unit Project Big Event you helped plan and set up—your vision of an undersea nature lodge, the "moving picture" you helped create, and all the ways you devised to tell the story of the ocean. What did you think was the most effective part of your group's presentation?

____

____

____

____

Which group's undersea nature lodge do you think would be most interesting to visit in real life? Explain why.

____

____

____

____

What did you learn about the ocean in watching other groups' presentations that you think you'll never forget.

____

____

____

How could pollution ruin the visions of the undersea lodges that you and your classmates presented?

____

____

____

UNIT F

Name_____________________________ Date_________

FORCES AND MOTION

In Unit F you'll learn about properties and measurements of forces and motion. For the Unit Project Big Event, you'll help build a miniature amusement park for marbles to demonstrate the laws of motion. What's your favorite ride at an amusement park?

____

What kind of motions does this ride put you through and how fast do you go?

____

____

____

If you were to design an amusement park, what kinds of motions would you make sure people could experience on rides?

____

____

____

Are there any rides you've been on that involve water in some way? Describe them.

____

____

At your favorite amusement park, are there any rides on which you can see the whole park? Describe them.

____

____

____

List the rides that you would include if you were to design your own park.

____

____

____

Name____ Date____________

UNIT PREVIEW

Consider what you already know about forces and motion, their properties, and how they can be measured. What else would you like to learn about these topics? List your ideas on the lines below.

CHAPTER PREVIEW

Name _______________________________ Date __________

MOVING ON

What if we measured things in pencil widths and pencil lengths? Measure each of the objects on this page in pencil widths or lengths and write the measurements you make beside the objects. Then make a line exactly one pencil length and three pencil widths down the right side of the page.

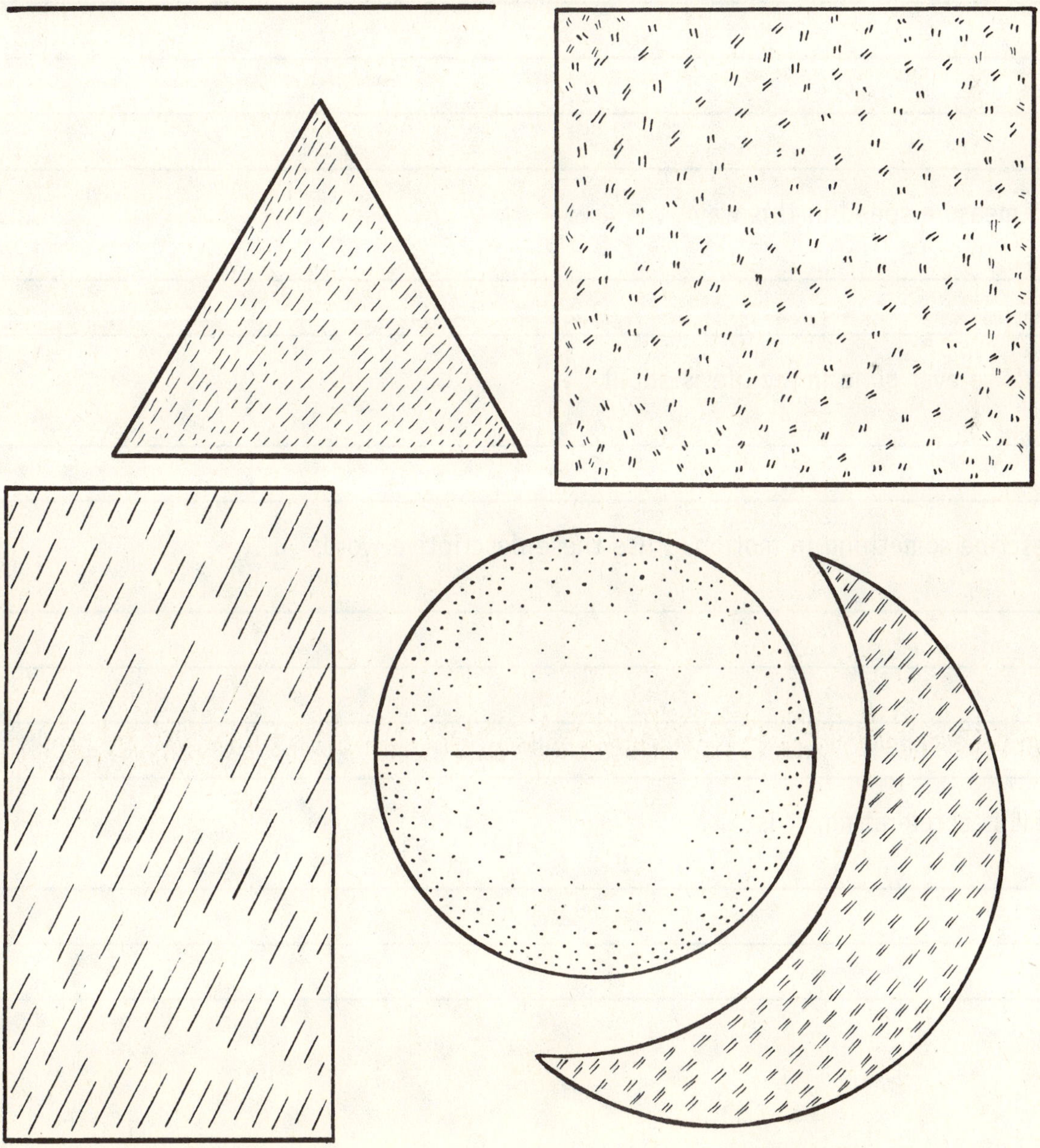

Name _______________________________ Date _____________

Dear Journal,

The units of measure I might use in a day include . . .

____

____

____

____

This is how I measure the motion of something . . .

____

____

____

____

We usually measure speed in this way . . .

____

____

The fastest I've ever gone in my life is about . . .

____

____

When I describe something in motion, I use these descriptive words . . .

____

____

____

____

If an object is accelerating, it is . . .

____

____

____

Name _______________________________ Date _____________

THE ANT MAZE

Procedure

Make a drawing of the path your ant will follow on a piece of graph paper. Keep this piece of graph paper in your *Science Notebook*.

Write your description of the ant's path, indicating distance and compass direction for each part of the path.

____

____

____

____

Analyze and Conclude

Write the answers to the questions in your book on the lines below.

1. ____

____

____

2. ____

____

____

3. ____

4. ____

____

____

____

Name ___________________________________ Date __________

Record your compass directions and distance measurements in meters to a specific place in your school or on the playground.

Describe how well your classmate was able to follow your directions to the place.

INVESTIGATION CLOSE

INVESTIGATION 1

1. Write directions from your school to your home. What two factors must be contained in your directions?

____

____

____

____

____

2. How does having a set of standards make a system of measurement more reliable?

____

____

____

____

____

For each thing in the list below, write the unit of measure most commonly used for it.

soda pop in a large bottle	__________	water in a pool	__________
weight of a person	__________	length of a person's life	__________
length of a baseball bat	__________	strength of a light bulb	__________
amount of flour in a recipe	__________	speed of a car	__________
temperature of air	__________	area of a farmer's field	__________
mass of an aspirin tablet	__________	length of a movie	__________
time of day	__________	truckload of apples	__________
length of a football field	__________	time of year	__________

Name _______________________________ Date __________

SPEEDING MARBLES

Procedure

Make a chart in the space below like the one on page F13. Each time you roll the marble at the wall, **record the time** it takes to reach the wall and then **calculate its speed**.

Write your prediction before the second three trials of how the elapsed time will vary as the speed of the marble is changed.

____

____

____

Analyze and Conclude

Write the answers to the questions in your book on the lines below.

1. ____

____

____

ACTIVITY RECORD

Name _______________________ Date _______________

2. ____

____

____

3. ____

____

____

4. ____

____

____

Record which ride at an amusement park is the fastest.

Record the speed of that ride at its fastest.

Record the names of the sources from which you got your information.

Name _______________________________ **Date** __________

INVESTIGATION 2

1. If you want to measure the speed of a car, what two factors do you need to know?

____

____

2. Approaching you is a car that appears to be traveling very fast. How might you figure out the speed of the car?

____

____

____

____

Determine the average speed in each case below:

A woman jogs 3 miles in 20 minutes, walks 1.5 miles in 30 minutes, and then finishes by jogging another 1.5 miles in 10 minutes. What was her average speed?

A driver on the highway travels 54 miles the first hour but then has to drive through a construction area. In the second hour, he only travels 36 miles. What was his average speed?

ACTIVITY RECORD

Name _______________________________ Date _____________

SWINGING SPEEDS

Procedure

Write your prediction of how the speed of the washer will change as it swings back and forth.

____

____

____

Record your observations of how the speed of the washer changes as it swings back and forth.

____

____

____

Make a drawing of the washer swinging. Label the place where it has the greatest speed and the place where it is traveling the slowest.

Name _______________________________________ Date ____________

Analyze and Conclude

Write the answers to the questions in your book on the lines below.

1. ____

____

____

2. ____

____

____

3. ____

____

____

4. ____

____

____

____

UNIT
F

Name_________________________________ Date__________

UNIT PROJECT LINK

Identify the amusement rides you want to have in Marble Park.

____

____

____

____

What else could you build to make this look like a real amusement park?

____

____

____

Make a drawing in the space below or on another piece of paper of how a tiny chair lift for marbles might be constructed.

In the space below or on another piece of paper, make a rough sketch of the Marble Park as you envision it.

Share this information with your group.

Name ___________________________ Date ___________

TWIN PENDULUMS

Procedure

Write your prediction of what would happen to the still pendulum if you released it while the other pendulum is moving.

____

____

____

Record your observations of what happens to the second pendulum when you pull back one pendulum and release it.

____

____

____

Record your observations the second time you try the experiment.

____

____

____

Record your observations the third time you try the experiment.

____

____

____

____

Analyze and Conclude

Write the answers to the questions in your book on the lines below.

1. ____

____

2. ____

____

ACTIVITY RECORD

CHAPTER 1

Name _______________________________________ Date _____________

3. ____

____

____

4. ____

____

____

Describe what astronauts experience during launch and reentry.

Describe how these experiences are related to acceleration.

Describe the effect that deceleration during reentry has on the space shuttle.

Record the names of the sources you used in your research.

Name ______________________________ Date __________

INVESTIGATION 3

1. When is an object accelerating?

____

____

____

2. You observe a ball bouncing down a long staircase. In what ways is the ball accelerating?

____

____

____

____

Make a flow chart to show what happens when a driver steps on the brake pedal.

CHAPTER WRAP-UP

Name _______________________________________ Date ___________

MOVING ON

How do you describe motion?

____

____

____

What are the two main systems of measurement used in the United
States? Which is used for scientific measurement?

____

____

____

____

What is speed and how is it measured?

____

____

____

____

What is the difference between velocity and acceleration?

____

____

____

____

How is deceleration related to acceleration? Explain your answer.

____

____

____

____

Name ___________________________________ Date ___________

Think about what you learned in Chapter 1 when you answer the following questions.

1. What was the most surprising thing you learned about motion as you read "Moving On"?

____

____

____

____

____

2. How did reading the chapter change your thinking about units of measure?

____

____

____

____

____

3. What did you learn about speed that you never knew before?

____

____

____

____

____

4. The next time you are riding in a car that is speeding up, what scientific thoughts might you think?

____

____

____

____

____

Name _________________________________ Date _________

GETTING A GRIP ON GRAVITY

What happens if you jump out of a plane—which way will you go? How
can you land safely? Draw people who have already jumped from this
plane and expect to land safely.

Name _________________________________ Date __________

Dear Journal,

I think the people on the other side of Earth don't fall off because . . .

____

____

____

The force of gravity on my body is described by this measurement . . .

____

____

____

If I dropped a marble and a large boulder off the roof of the school, at the same time, they would hit ground . . .

____

____

____

A person jumping off a high dive makes a bigger splash than a person jumping off a low dive because . . .

____

____

____

If I were on the Moon, my weight would be changed because . . .

____

____

____

____

The reason why parachutes work is . . .

____

____

____

____

ACTIVITY RECORD

Name _________________________________ Date _________

MEASURING GRAVITY'S PULL

Procedure

Make a chart in the space below like the one on page F31. Your chart should be big enough to record the mass of all the objects you have plus one more, your body.

Record your measurements of mass and force of gravity for every object you have. Use a separate sheet of paper to make your calculations of the ratio of gravity to mass for each object. Keep this sheet in your *Science Notebook*.

Analyze and Conclude

Write the answers to the questions in your book on the lines below.

1. ____

____

2. ____

____

____

3. ____

____

____

Name _______________________________________ Date _____________

Describe the design of the scale you have invented.

INVESTIGATE FURTHER!

EXPERIMENT

Page F31

Sketch your design in the space below.

Describe how successful your design was in getting readings similar to those obtained with the spring scale.

INVESTIGATION 1

1. What is the difference between mass and weight?

____

____

____

____

2. Your 400 gold coins were stolen, but the police have found them in Death Valley. When asked how much your gold weighs, you answer, "980 newtons." The officer says, "Sorry, this gold weighs more than that." What has happened?

____

____

____

____

You look up the metric system in a reference book and you discover that it says "1 kg = 2.2046 lbs." On the lines below, explain why that equation really doesn't make sense but usually works out anyway.

____

____

____

____

Name _________________________________ Date _________

THE GREAT GRAVITY RACE

Procedure

Record your measurement of the weight of the heavier ball.

____

Record your measurement of the weight of the lighter ball.

____

Write your prediction of which ball will hit the ground first if they both roll off the table together.

____

____

Record your observations of which ball hits the ground first when they both roll off the table together.

____

____

Record your observations for each time you repeat the activity. Try it five more times.

1. ____

____

2. ____

____

3. ____

____

4. ____

____

5. ____

____

Name _________________________________ Date __________

Make two sketches to show what you observe when you roll the balls off the table together.

Analyze and Conclude

Write the answers to the questions in your book on the lines below.

1. ____

____

____

2. ____

____

____

Name _______________________________ Date __________

FALLING TOGETHER

Procedure

Write your prediction of which penny will hit the ground first if you flick the long edges of the card with your finger.

____

____

Record your observations of which penny hits the ground first when you flick the long edges of the card with your finger.

____

____

Record your observations for each of the three more times you repeat the experiment with the pennies.

1. ____

____

2. ____

____

3. ____

____

Write your prediction of whether the penny or the quarter will hit the ground first if you flick the card with your finger.

____

____

Record your observations of whether the penny or the quarter hits the ground first when you flick the card with your finger.

____

____

ACTIVITY RECORD

Name _________________________________ Date _________

Write your prediction of whether the penny or the quarter will hit the ground first if the quarter is in the other position.

____

____

____

Record your observations of whether the penny or the quarter hits the ground first when the quarter is in the other position.

____

____

Analyze and Conclude

Write the answers to the questions in your book on the lines below.

1. ____

2. ____

3. ____

Record the pairs of objects you dropped in your experiment.

Describe the results you observed.

Infer from your results whether the weight of a falling object has an effect on the rate of its fall.

Name_________________________________ Date__________

UNIT PROJECT LINK

Describe your design for one of your roller coasters. Make sure you clearly state what materials you will use in your design.

____

____

____

____

Sketch your design in the space below or on another piece of paper. Write the name of this roller coaster below the sketch.

Describe your design for the second of your roller coasters.

Sketch your second design in the space below or on another piece of paper. Write the name of this roller coaster below the sketch.

Share this information with your group.

Name ____ Date _____________

INVESTIGATION 2

1. Would the graph on page F40 be useful in predicting the fall of both a marble and a baseball? Why or why not?

____

____

____

2. An astronaut standing on the Moon and a scientist standing on Earth drop identical hammers from identical heights at exactly the same moment. Which will hit the ground first? Explain your answer.

____

____

____

____

Imagine that you're Galileo, and hundreds of years ago you decide to test the rate at which objects fall. Write an entry in your journal describing your experiment, the results, and how those results have changed your thinking. Make sure you first write the date and place of the experiment.

Galileo's Journal

____

____

____

____

____

____

____

____

Name _______________________________ Date _________

PAPER RACE

Procedure

Make a chart in the space below similar to the one on page F42, though you will need to make it longer. Repeat *Crumpled paper* and *Flat paper* three more times. **Record the weight** of both the crumpled sheet and the flat sheet on your chart each time you do the experiment.

Write your prediction of what will happen if both sheets of paper are dropped from the same height at the same time.

____

____

____

____

Record your observations in your chart of what happens when both sheets of paper are dropped from the same height at the same time. Then repeat the experiment three more times, recording your results in the chart each time.

Name _______________________________ Date _______________

Analyze and Conclude

Write the answers to the questions in your book on the lines below.

1. ____
____

2. ____
____

3. ____
____

Sketch the different shapes of seeds you tested.

Describe from what you observed how the different seed shapes affect their rates of fall.

Infer how these different rates could be advantageous for the trees.

Name _______________________________ Date _______

PARACHUTING

Procedure

Make a chart in the space below similar to the one on page F44. But make your chart longer: repeat *Small parachute* three more times, and then repeat *Large parachute* three more times. Do the experiment with the small parachute first. Each time you drop the action figure, **record the height** of the drop and the drop time in your chart.

Write your prediction of how drops of the action figure with the large parachute will compare with the drops of the action figure with the small parachute.

____

____

Record the height of the drop and the drop time in your chart each time you drop the action figure using the large parachute.

ACTIVITY RECORD

Name ___________________________ Date _________

Analyze and Conclude

Write the answers to the questions in your book on the lines below.

1. ____
____
____
____

2. ____
____
____

3. ____
____

INVESTIGATE FURTHER!

EXPERIMENT

Page F45

Describe the angles you tilted the fan when you repeated the activity.

Record your observations of how the fan affected the fall of the action figures with the parachutes.

Tell whether your observations support your explanation of how a parachute works.

Name _________________________________ Date __________

INVESTIGATION 3

1. Could you sky-dive on the Moon? Why or why not?

____

____

____

2. Sky divers sometimes try to make themselves fall faster. What can they do to make themselves fall faster?

____

____

____

____

In the space below, draw a parachutist with an open parachute. Then use arrows and labels to show the forces acting on the parachute.

CHAPTER WRAP-UP

Name _______________________________ Date __________

GETTING A GRIP ON GRAVITY

What is gravity and how can the pull of Earth's gravity on objects be measured?

____

____

____

____

What is the difference between mass and weight?

____

____

____

____

Do things fall at the same rate? Explain your answer.

____

____

____

____

How can the rate at which an object falls be changed? Give an example.

____

____

____

____

Why would a feather fall at the same rate as a hammer on the Moon?

____

____

____

____

Name ____ Date __________

Think about what you learned in Chapter 2 when you answer the following questions.

1. What did you learn about falling objects that surprised you most?

____

____

____

____

____

____

2. What did you learn as you read "Getting a Grip on Gravity" that you're still not sure you understand?

____

____

____

____

____

____

3. Did reading the chapter make you more or less fearful of jumping from a plane with a parachute? Give reasons for your feeling.

____

____

____

____

____

____

Name ___________________________ Date __________

MAKING AND MEASURING MOTION

In the boxes below, draw two ways this bicyclist could stop his bike.

Name _________________________________ Date _________

Dear Journal,

When I push someone on a swing, I have to push hardest . . .

____

____

When I'm riding in a car, I'm jerked back when . . .

____

____

____

If I need to hammer a big nail, I use a big hammer because . . .

____

____

____

I think a baseball flies farther when the batter swings the bat faster
because . . .

____

____

____

Friction is . . .

____

____

____

Friction can be a problem when . . .

____

____

____

____

CHAPTER
3

Name ______________________________ Date __________

RIDER MOVES

Procedure

Make a drawing in the space below of how you have set up the trucks and the block.

Write your prediction of what will happen if you hit the first truck sharply from behind.

____

____

____

Record your observations of what happens when you hit the first truck sharply from behind.

____

____

____

Add labels and arrows to your drawing above to show what happens when you hit the first truck sharply from behind.

Record your observations of what happens as you repeat the activity twice to be sure of your results.

____

____

____

Name _________________________________ Date _________

Record your observations of what happens when you use the second truck to hit the first truck from the front.

____

____

____

Analyze and Conclude

Write the answers to the questions in your book on the lines below.

1. _______________________________________

____

2. _______________________________________

____

3. _______________________________________

____

____

Describe the "passengers" you used in your experiments.

Does the shape of the passenger have any effect on the outcome?

Does the material from which the passenger is made have any effect on the outcome?

ACTIVITY RECORD

Name _________________________________ Date _________

CRASH-TEST DUMMIES

Procedure

Record your observations of what happens to your crash-test dummy as a result of the truck's collision with the wall.

____

____

____

Record your observations when you repeat the activity using improved safety equipment.

____

____

____

Record your observations of what happens to your crash-test dummy when you repeat the test with the ramp made steeper.

____

____

____

Analyze and Conclude

Write the answers to the questions in your book on the lines below.

1. ____

____

____

2. ____

____

____

Name ___________________________ Date ___________

3. ____
____
____

4. ____
____
____

5. ____
____
____
____
____

INVESTIGATE FURTHER!

RESEARCH

Page F57

Describe the safety precautions that amusement parks use on loop rides.

Record the names of the sources you used in your research.

Name _______________________________________ Date ____________

INVESTIGATION 1

1. Compare two cars in terms of inertia. One is sitting in the driveway; the other is rolling along a level street.

____

____

____

____

2. As you come around a corner, you run into a table and a crystal vase tips toward you. You reach out in desperation and catch it before it hits the table. What made the vase tip? Why did it tip toward you and not away from you?

____

____

____

____

When you're in a moving car, you and everything else in the car is moving forward with the car. What if you drop a ball out the window of a moving car? The ball has inertia. Make a sketch in the space below that shows a car moving from the left side of the page to the right side. Use a dotted line to show the path of a ball that is dropped out the window on the left side of the page.

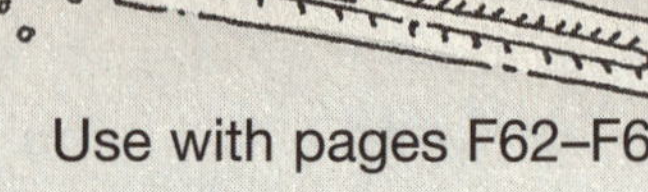

Name _________________________________ Date __________

STARTING AND STOPPING

Procedure

Write your prediction of the direction in which the ball will move if you gently push it with the crayon.

____

____

Record your observations of the path in which the ball moves when you gently push it with the crayon.

____

____

____

Write your prediction of the direction in which the ball will move if you forcefully push it with the crayon.

____

____

Record your observations of the path in which the ball moves when you forcefully push it with the crayon.

____

____

____

Write your prediction of the direction in which the ball will move when you gently strike the ball with the crayon over the second line.

____

____

Record your observations of the path in which the ball moves when you gently strike it with the crayon over the second line.

____

____

____

CHAPTER 3

Name _____________________________________ Date __________

Analyze and Conclude

Write the answers to the questions in your book on the lines below.

1. ____

____

____

2. ____

____

____

INVESTIGATE FURTHER!

EXPERIMENT

Page F63

Describe what you have to do to a soccer ball to make it curve as it moves away from you.

Sketch how you would kick a soccer ball to make it curve as it moves away from you.

Describe how you would have to kick a soccer ball to make it spin backward.

Sketch how you would make a soccer ball spin backward.

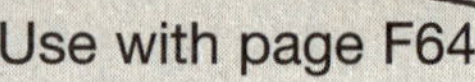

Name _______________________________________ Date __________

THE PROBLEM WITH BIG TRUCKS

Procedure

Write your prediction of how the trucks will move if you apply equal force to each.

____

____

Make a chart in the space below to record your measurements of how far each truck moves when you apply equal force to each. Make your chart four columns wide. In the first column, describe the two trucks. In the second column, **record the distance** each truck moves in your first trial. **Record the distances** you measure in the next two trials in the final two columns.

Make your calculations of the average distance each truck moved in the space below. For each truck, add the three distances and then divide by 3.

Record your measurement of the distance the lighter truck travels after hitting the block.

____

Record your measurement of the distance the heavier truck travels after hitting the block.

____

Name _________________________________ Date __________

Analyze and Conclude

Write the answers to the questions in your book on the lines below.

1. ____

____

2. ____

____

3. ____

____

____

Describe the lightest car and the heaviest truck you
found in your research.

Compare the two vehicles in terms of their engines and brake
systems.

Infer the reasons for the differences you found in the engines
and the brakes of the two vehicles.

Name _________________________________ Date __________

INVESTIGATION 2

1. What can you infer about the force necessary to throw a ball with an acceleration of 5 m/s^2 compared with the force required to throw it at 10 m/s^2?

____

____

____

2. A wagon has a mass of 20 kg. One child has a mass of 30 kg while another has a mass of 40 kg. A third child pushes the wagon. What force is needed to accelerate each child plus the wagon to 5 m/s^2?

____

____

____

____

Consider two baseball players, both of whom want to hit more home runs. Therefore each player thinks, "I need a swing of the bat that has more force to it." But the two players decide on different ways to achieve the same goal. One player switches to a heavier bat, one with more mass. The other player switches to a lighter bat, one with less mass. Think of the formula for force, and then explain how each player is planning to make a more forceful swing.

____

____

____

____

____

____

Name ___________________________ Date __________

FRICTION FLOORS

Procedure

Make a chart in the space below to record the distances traveled by the toy car over various materials. For each of the four materials, you will need to make spaces to record the distances for three trials.

Record the distances in your chart each time you make your measurement of how far the car travels on a material.

Analyze and Conclude

Write the answers to the questions in your book on the lines below.

1. ____

____

2. ____

____

____

3. ____

____

____

____

Name _______________________________ Date _______________

INVESTIGATE FURTHER!

EXPERIMENT

Page F71

List the materials you tested to make the ice less slippery.

Describe how you conducted your tests on these materials.

Record how effective the materials you tested were.

Name _________________________________ Date __________

WHEEL POWER

Procedure

Record your observations of what happens when you release the truck on the ramp.

____

____

____

____

Record your observations of what happens when you release the box on the ramp.

____

____

____

____

Analyze and Conclude

Write the answers to the questions in your book on the lines below.

1. ____

____

____

____

2. ____

____

____

____

Name _______________________________ Date __________

Describe how ball bearings reduce friction.

INVESTIGATE FURTHER!

RESEARCH

Page F72

Where have you found ball bearings in use?

Describe some liquid substances you have found that reduce the friction between moving objects.

UNIT PROJECT LINK

UNIT F

Unit Project Link

Describe your design for one of the motion rides you would like to build. This ride should start, stop, and carry at least one marble. Design this ride to turn in circles. Make sure you clearly state what materials you will use in your design.

____

____

____

Sketch your design in the space below or on another piece of paper. Write the name of this ride below your sketch.

Describe a second design of a ride that starts, stops, and carries at least one marble. Design this ride to use a swing. Make sure you clearly state what materials you will use in your design.

____

____

____

Sketch your second design in the space below or on another piece of paper. Write the name of this ride below your sketch.

Share this information with your group.

Name _______________________________________ Date __________

INVESTIGATION 3

1. How does friction help the movement of a car? How does friction hinder the movement of the car?

____

____

____

____

2. During the winter, highway department road crews often spread sand or cinders on ice. Why do they do this?

____

____

____

____

Make a drawing in the space below of the bottom of one of the shoes you have on. Then, on the lines, infer from that surface whether your shoe was designed to increase friction a little or a great deal.

____

____

____

Name _______________________________________ Date ____________

MAKING AND MEASURING MOTION

How are objects at rest and objects in motion alike?

____

____

What is Newton's First Law of Motion?

____

____

____

____

How do forces affect motion?

____

____

____

What is Newton's Second Law of Motion?

____

____

____

____

Write the mathematical formula that shows how force causes a change in
the speed or direction of an object.

____

____

What is friction and how does it affect the motion of objects?

____

____

____

____

Name _________________________________ Date _____________

Think about what you learned in Chapter 3 when you answer the following questions.

1. What did you find most interesting as you read "Making and Measuring Motion"?

____

____

____

____

____

2. What was the most difficult concept for you to understand about the motion of objects?

____

____

____

____

____

3. What did you learn in reading the chapter that might prove useful in your everyday life?

____

____

____

____

____

4. Describe something you learned about motion that you think you'll never forget.

____

____

____

____

____

Name _______________________________ Date _________

FORCES IN PAIRS

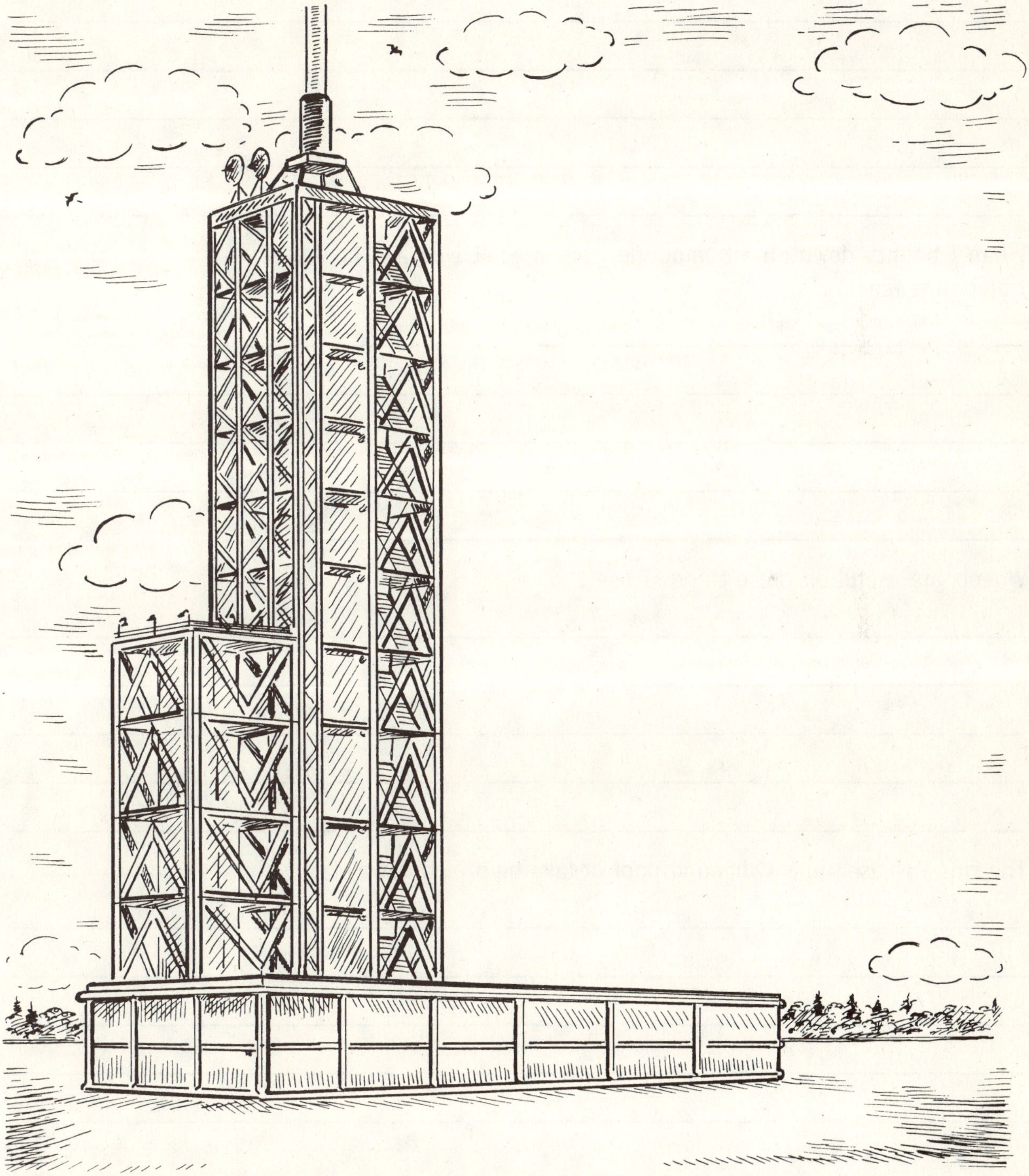

"Ten, nine, eight, seven, six, five, four, ignition, three, two, one . . . we have liftoff." Draw a rocket at launch, with its engines blasting away.

Name _______________________________ Date __________

Dear Journal,

When one ball collides with another . . .

____

____

____

____

When I bounce down on a trampoline, this is what I do and how the trampoline reacts . . .

____

____

____

____

Wheels are useful on these things I use . . .

____

____

____

____

The fins I've used in a swimming pool or lake help in this way . . .

____

____

____

____

Name ___________________________________ Date ___________

MARBLE COLLISIONS

Procedure

Write your prediction of what will happen when a large moving marble collides with a small stationary marble.

____

Record your observations of what happens when a large moving marble collides with a small stationary marble.

____

Write your prediction of what will happen when a large moving marble collides with a small moving marble.

____

Record your observations of what happens when a large moving marble collides with a small moving marble.

____

Write your prediction of what will happen when a large moving marble collides with a large moving marble.

____

Record your observations of what happens when a large moving marble collides with a large moving marble.

____

Write your prediction of what will happen when a large moving marble collides with the first marble in a row of two small stationary marbles.

____

Record your observations of what happens when a large moving marble collides with the first marble in a row of two small stationary marbles.

____

Write your prediction of what will happen when a small moving marble collides with a small stationary marble.

____

Name _______________________________________ Date __________

Record your observations of what happens when a small moving marble collides with a small stationary marble.

____

Write your prediction of what will happen if a small moving marble collides with a small moving marble.

____

Record your observations of what happens when a small moving marble collides with a small moving marble.

____

Write your prediction of what will happen when a small moving marble collides with a large moving marble.

____

Record your observations of what happens when a small moving marble collides with a large moving marble.

____

Write your prediction or what will happen when a small moving marble collides with a small stationary marble that is directly in front of, and touching, a large stationary marble.

____

Record your observations of what happens when a small moving marble collides with a small stationary marble that is directly in front of, and touching, a large stationary marble.

____

Analyze and Conclude

Write the answers to the questions in your book on the lines below.

1. ____

____

____

____

ACTIVITY RECORD

CHAPTER **4**

Name _________________________ Date __________

2. _______________________________________
____
____

3. _______________________________________
____
____
____

4. _______________________________________
____
____
____

Predict which ball, the beach ball or the basketball, will have the greater momentum.

Describe your experiment and findings.

Infer from your experiment the two things momentum depends on.

Use with pages F82–F83.

Name _______________________________ Date _____________

FOOTBALL MOMENTUM

Procedure

Record your observations of what happens after the collision of the big marble and the small marble, each rolling at the same speed.

____

____

Record your observations of what happens after the collision of the small marble and the large marble when the small marble is going twice as fast.

____

____

Record your observations of what happens after the collision when the large marble rolls into the small marble at rest.

____

____

Analyze and Conclude

Write the answers to the questions in your book on the lines below.

1. ____

____

2. ____

____

3. ____

____

4. ____

____

Name_______________________________ Date__________

Unit Project Link

Describe your experiences with bumper cars at an amusement park.

____

____

____

____

Imagine two bumper cars racing toward each other and colliding.
Describe what you think would happen after the collision.

____

____

____

____

What do you think happens when a fast-moving car slams into a
car that isn't moving?

____

____

____

____

What do you think happens when one bumper car hits another
bumper car that is touching a third bumper car?

____

____

____

____

Use marbles of the same size as models for bumper cars to create a
variety of collisions involving two or three bumper cars. For each
collision, write a description of what happens and make a drawing
of it on an index card. Keep these cards in your *Science Notebook*.

Share this information with your group.

Name _______________________________ Date __________

INVESTIGATION 1

1. A cue ball rolls quickly toward the racked pool balls. Colliding with the first ball in the triangle, the cue ball comes to a complete stop. The racked pool balls, however, scatter in all directions. Explain what has happened in terms of conservation of momentum.

____

____

____

____

2. Explain how conservation of momentum is involved in table tennis.

____

____

____

____

Suppose a child, whose mass is 16 kg, is on a bicycle with a mass of 4 kg. The child is pedaling hard and has reached a speed of 8 m/s. What is the momentum of the child and bike together? Make a sketch of the child and bike, with labels to show the mass of each, the speed, and the momentum.

ACTIVITY RECORD

CHAPTER 4

Name _______________________________________ Date ____________

BOUNCING BALLS

Procedure

Record your observations of the bouncing ball. At which point is the ball traveling the fastest and at which point is it traveling the slowest?

____

____

____

Record your observations of the ball's direction. At which point does the ball's motion change direction?

____

____

____

Write your prediction of what will happen when you bounce the ball harder against the floor.

____

____

Record your observations of what happens when you bounce the ball harder against the floor.

____

____

Analyze and Conclude

Write the answers to the question in your book on the lines below.

1. ____

2. ____

____

3. ____

____

____

Compare the bounces of the two balls you dropped from different heights.

Compare the speeds of the two balls you dropped from different heights.

Infer from your observations the relationship between the force of the ball's hitting the floor and the floor's pushing against the ball.

Infer from your observations the relationship between the speed of the ball hitting the floor and the speed of the ball as it bounces upward.

ACTIVITY RECORD

Name _________________________________ Date __________

DOUBLE-BALL BOUNCE

Procedure

Record your observations of what happens when you drop a clay ball onto the floor.

____

____

Make a drawing of what happens when you drop the basketball with the clay ball on top. Draw the location of the clay ball when the basketball hits the ground, and draw the path of the clay ball after the basketball has hit the floor and rebounded.

Record your observations of how high the basketball bounced when it was dropped with the clay ball on top of it.

____

Write your prediction of how high the basketball will bounce without the clay ball on top of it.

____

Record your observations of how high the basketball bounces when it is dropped without the clay ball on top of it.

____

____

Name _______________________________ Date __________

Analyze and Conclude

Write the answers to the questions in your book on the lines below.

1. ____

____

2. ____

____

3. ____

____

____

4. ____

____

____

Describe your design of how you could make rockets
sail across the room using a basketball as the launcher.

Infer from your experiment what happens in this series of events
in terms of actions and reactions.

Name _________________________________ Date __________

INVESTIGATION 2

1. Imagine a girl on a pair of in-line skates. She faces a brick wall and pushes forcefully on the wall. Explain what happens in terms of actions and reactions.

____

____

____

____

2. When a rocket lifts off a launch pad, where is the action force and where is the reaction force? Think! When the rocket is 2.2 km (1 mi) off the launch pad, where are the action and reaction forces?

____

____

____

____

Make a sketch of a student jumping rope, with feet just off the floor and knees bent (the student has just flown into the air). The momentum of the student is 500 kg x m/s. On your sketch, label the action force and the reaction force, using arrows. Also label the momentum of the student and Earth with arrows, showing the value of the momentum of each.

Name _______________________________ Date __________

ACTION-REACTION WHEELS

Procedure

Write your prediction of which way the spinning wheels of the wind-up
car will push your hand when you touch them.

____

____

Record your observations of which way the spinning wheels push your
hand when you touch them.

____

____

Make a drawing of the car resting on the table. With arrows, show the
direction the car traveled and the way the wheels push on the ground.

Analyze and Conclude

Write the answers to the questions in your book on the lines below.

1. ____

____

2. ____

____

____

INVESTIGATE FURTHER

Name _________________________________ Date __________

Describe what happens when you run the car on a soft pillow.

Describe what happens when you run the car on carpet or tile.

Infer from your observations why the surface underneath the car is important to how well it runs.

Name ____ Date ____________

INVESTIGATION 3

1. Draw a car and its wheels. Diagram the action force and the reaction force needed for the car to go forward. Diagram the action force and the reaction force needed for the car to go backward.

2. You use action-reaction forces all the time. Explain how action-reaction forces affect you when you walk, climb stairs, roll over, or do a push-up.

____

____

____

____

Make a flow chart in the space below that shows the series of action forces and reaction forces that propel a diver with swim fins through the water. Your flow chart should include an up-and-down movement of the right leg and an up-and-down movement of the left leg. Label each step in the chart either an action force or a reaction force.

CHAPTER WRAP-UP

Name _______________________________________ Date ____________

FORCES IN PAIRS

What property do all moving objects share?

____

____

____

What is the mathematical formula for momentum?

____

State the Law of Conservation of Momentum.

____

____

What is Newton's Third Law of Motion?

____

____

When you push against the floor, what is the cause of the jump that results?

____

____

____

Describe how a wheel uses action-reaction forces to move forward.

____

____

____

____

What is the main advantage of using the wheel?

____

____

____

____

CHAPTER WRAP-UP

Name _________________________________ Date __________

Think about what you learned in Chapter 4 when you answer the following questions.

1. What surprised you most as you read "Forces in Pairs"?

____

____

____

____

____

2. On page 367 you drew a rocket blasting off. How have your thoughts about this changed now that you've read the chapter?

____

____

____

____

____

3. What was the most useful thing you learned in reading about pairs of forces?

____

____

____

____

____

4. What did you find most difficult to understand in reading about forces in pairs? What could you do to understand it better?

____

____

____

____

____

Name ________________________________   Date ____________

REAL-WORLD FORCES

Draw two planes in this sky. Draw one plane that is powered by propellers. Draw another plane that is powered by jet engines.

Use with pages F104–F105.

Name _______________________________ Date __________

Dear Journal,

These are the experiences I've had with planes . . .

____

____

____

____

An airplane is able to take off and fly because . . .

____

____

____

____

A rocket can lift off and fly because . . .

____

____

____

____

____

This is how I can float in water . . .

____

____

____

____

This is why large boats float in the water . . .

____

____

____

____

Name _________________________________ Date __________

MAKING A PAPER GLIDER

Procedure

Write your prediction of how your airplane will fly.

____

____

____

Make a chart in the space below like the one on page F107. Each time
you test your airplane, **record the results** of the test in your chart.

Analyze and Conclude

Write the answers to the questions in your book on the lines below.

1. ____

____

____

2. ____

____

____

Name _______________________________ Date __________

3. ____

____

4. ____

____

____

5. ____

____

____

INVESTIGATE FURTHER!
· · · · · · · · · · · · · · ·
EXPERIMENT

Page F107

Describe the design of the airplane you made.

Describe your results with the airplane you designed. How well did it fly?

Describe the best-designed airplane among all the ones you and your classmates made. Why do you think it flew the best?

ACTIVITY RECORD

Name _______________________________ Date __________

PROPELLER POWER!

Procedure

Write your prediction of what will happen when you drop the two spinners from the same height.

____

____

____

____

Record your observations of what happens when you drop the two spinners from the same height.

____

____

____

____

Write your prediction of what will happen when you repeat step 3.

____

____

____

Record your observations of what happens when you repeat step 3.

____

____

____

____

Name _________________________________ Date _________

Write your prediction of what will happen when you drop the two narrow spinners from the same height.

____

____

____

____

Record your observations of what happens when you drop the two narrow spinners from the same height.

____

____

____

____

____

Analyze and Conclude

Write the answers to the questions in your book on the lines below.

1. ____

____

____

2. ____

____

3. ____

____

Name _________________________________ Date __________

INVESTIGATION 1

1. Make a drawing that shows and describes the forces acting on an airplane in flight.

2. Explain why the wings of a space shuttle are absolutely useless for most of its mission.

____

____

____

____

Look at the drawing of the one of the Wright brothers' planes on page F109. What can you see in the design of that plane that has been greatly improved in modern planes? Give reasons for your answer.

____

____

____

____

____

Name ______________________________ Date __________

BALLOON ROCKET RACE

Procedure

Write your prediction of what will happen if you release the end of the balloon after you've taped it to the straw.

____

____

Record your observations of what happens when you release the end of the balloon.

____

____

Record your measurement of how far the balloon traveled on the string.

____

Record your observations of what happens when you repeat the activity with the balloon inflated as big as you can make it.

____

____

Record your measurement of how far the balloon traveled when you repeated the activity.

____

Analyze and Conclude

1.–2. Make your drawing in the space below.

ACTIVITY RECORD

Name _________________________________ Date _________

Write the answers to the questions in your book on the lines below.

3. ____

____

4. ____

____

____

____

Draw the shapes of several balloons you tried in the balloon race. Beside each shape, **record the distance** that balloon traveled along the string.

What conclusions can you make from the results of your experiment?

Name _______________________________ Date _________

STRAW ROCKETS

Procedure

Write your prediction of what will happen if you release the air from the balloon.

____

____

Record your observations of what happens when you release the air from the balloon.

____

____

____

Analyze and Conclude

Make your drawing in the space below.

1.–3.

Write the answer to the question in your book on the lines below.

4. ______________________________________

____

____

____

INVESTIGATE FURTHER

Name ___________________________________ Date ___________

Predict what will happen if you uncover the holes in the water-filled milk carton.

Describe what happens when you uncover the holes in the water-filled milk carton.

Sketch in the space below what happens when you uncover the holes. Draw arrows in your sketch to show the action forces and reaction forces that result in the movement you observe.

Name _______________________________________ Date ___________

INVESTIGATION 2

1. How are action-reaction forces involved in launching a rocket?

____

____

____

____

2. How is blowing up a balloon and releasing it similar to launching a
rocket in terms of action-reaction forces?

____

____

____

____

In the space below, make a sketch of a jet airplane with one jet engine
in the rear. With labels and arrows, indicate the action force and the
reaction force that causes the necessary thrust for the plane to fly.

ACTIVITY RECORD

CHAPTER 5

Name ___________________________________ Date ___________

CLAY BOATS
· · · · · · · · · · · · · · · · · · ·

Procedure

Record your observations of what happens when you place the ball of clay in the water.

____

____

Record your observations of what happens when you place your clay boat in the water.

____

____

Make a drawing of your boat in the space below.

Write your prediction of what will happen when you add marbles to your boat.

____

____

Record the number of marbles that your boat held before it sank.

____

Make a drawing in the space below of your redesign of the boat.

Name _______________________________________ Date __________

Write your prediction of how many marbles your redesigned boat will hold before it sinks.

____

____

Record the number of marbles that your redesigned boat held before it sank.

____

Analyze and Conclude

Write the answers to the questions in your book on the lines below.

1. ____

____

____

____

2. ____

____

____

3. ____

____

____

____

4. ____

____

____

____

UNIT PROJECT LINK

UNIT **F**

Name_______________________________________ Date__________

UNIT PROJECT LINK

Describe a water ride you've seen at an amusement park.

____

____

Describe your design of a water ride for the Marble Park. Describe
the shape of the main structure and the boat, tell how many passengers the boat will carry, and estimate how fast the boat will
move. Make sure you clearly state what materials you will use in
your design.

____

____

____

____

Sketch your design in the space below or on another piece of
paper. Write the name of this water ride below the sketch.

What factors will affect the splash the boat makes in the splash
pool at the end?

____

Share this information with your group.

Name _______________________________ Date __________

FLOATING EGG

Procedure

Write your prediction of what will happen if you place an egg in the water.

____

____

Record your observations of what happens when you place an egg in the water.

____

____

Write your prediction of what will happen if you place an egg in the water after you have added salt.

____

____

Record your observations of what happens when you place an egg in the water after you have added salt.

____

____

Analyze and Conclude

Write the answers to the questions in your book on the lines below.

1. _______________________________________

____

2. _______________________________________

____

____

3. _______________________________________

____

INVESTIGATE FURTHER

Name _________________________________ Date _________

Describe what you discovered about swimming in the ocean.

Infer from your research why there is a difference in how easy it is to swim in ocean water as opposed to fresh water.

Record the names of the sources you used in your research.

Name _______________________________ Date _____________

INVESTIGATION 3

1. How are action-reaction forces involved when you are floating in a pool?

____

____

____

____

2. A submarine is said to not only float in the water but also to "fly" through the water. Explain how a submarine "flies" in terms of action-reaction forces.

____

____

____

____

____

Think back to the activity on pages F120 and F121. Now that you understand factors that affect buoyancy, explain why your clay boat floated and explain what you did when you added the marbles.

____

____

____

____

____

CHAPTER WRAP-UP

Name ____ Date ____________

REAL-WORLD FORCES

Describe the two forces that allow a heavy thing to fly.

____

____

____

____

Describe the two forces that work against a heavy thing flying.

____

____

____

____

What are the action-reaction forces in the launch of a rocket?

____

____

____

____

How are heavy objects able to float in water?

____

____

____

____

CHAPTER WRAP-UP

Name _______________________ Date _______________

Think about what you learned in Chapter 5 when you answer the following questions.

1. What did you find most interesting as you read "Real-World Forces?"

____

____

____

____

2. What did you learn about that changed your understanding of how airplanes can fly?

____

____

____

____

____

3. Do you think that if everyone understood the forces involved in flying fewer people would be so scared of airplanes? Explain your answer.

____

____

____

____

4. What did you read in the chapter that you still don't understand well? What could you do to understand it better?

____

____

____

____

Name_________________________________ Date__________

Unit Project Wrap-Up

Think about the Unit Project Big Event you helped create—the Marble Park—in which the rides demonstrated each of Newton's laws of motion. Which ride do you think best demonstrated Newton's First Law of Motion? Give reasons for your choice.

____

____

____

____

____

Which ride do you think best demonstrated Newton's Second Law of Motion? Give reasons for your choice.

____

____

____

____

____

Which ride do you think best demonstrated Newton's Third Law of Motion? Give reasons for you choice.

____

____

____

____

Which ride were you most proud to have been a part of creating? Tell why.

____

____

____

____

UNIT PREVIEW

Name_______________________________ Date________

GROWING UP HEALTHY

In Unit G you'll learn about the human life cycle, how your body protects itself against diseases, and how to make healthful choices in your life. For the Unit Project Big Event, you'll help plan and present a Healthful Consumer Fair through which you can educate families, friends, and other classes about the importance of being a healthful consumer. What do you think are the main things healthy people do to keep their health?

____

____

____

____

____

What are some specific things you do every day or week that you think contributes to your staying healthy?

____

____

____

____

____

What are some behaviors that you see among your friends and neighbors that you think most contributes to bad health?

____

____

____

____

Name_____________________________________ Date__________

UNIT PREVIEW

Consider what you already know about keeping your body healthy
and making healthful choices. What more would you like to learn?
Make a list of questions you have about staying healthy on the
lines below.

Name _________________________________ Date __________

THE HUMAN LIFE CYCLE

This mother and father each have some distinctive traits. Complete the picture to show what their child might look like.

Name _________________________________ Date __________

Dear Journal,

These are some traits I think were passed on to me from one or the other
of my parents . . .

____

____

____

____

____

The structures within cells responsible for passing on traits are . . .

____

____

Some diseases that can be inherited are . . .

____

____

____

____

To make sure the baby is born healthy, a pregnant woman should . . .

____

____

____

____

I think an adolescent is different from a child in these ways . . .

____

____

____

____

Name _______________________________________ Date ___________

OBSERVING TRAITS

Procedure

Record your inference about the difference between dominant and recessive traits.

____

____

____

Write your prediction of which variety of each trait will be most common among your classmates.

____

____

____

____

Make a chart in the space below to record how many students are dominant for each trait and how many are recessive for each trait. For each dominant or recessive variety, **record the number** of students who have that variety as well as the percentage of the class who have that variety.

Name _______________________________________ Date _____________

Make your calculations in the space below of the percentage of class members who have each trait.

Analyze and Conclude

Write the answers to the questions in your book on the lines below.

1. ____

____

____

____

____

2. ____

____

____

3. ____

____

____

INVESTIGATE FURTHER

Name ________________________________ Date __________

Make a chart in the space below like the one you made for the activity. Then survey the students in another classroom, the adults in the school, or some other group to investigate how common the varieties of these seven traits are.

Compare the percentages you found in your extended survey with the percentages in your classroom.

Use with page G8.

Name _______________________________________ Date _____________

BOY OR GIRL?

Procedure

Record the resulting combination of letters the first time you and your partner each flip a game piece.

____

Write your prediction of how many flips will result in boys and how many will result in girls.

____

____

____

Record the combination of letters each time you and your partner flip the game pieces. Write your first combination again next to number 1. Then you and your partner should flip the pieces 29 more times.

1. _____________	11. _____________	21. _____________
2. _____________	12. _____________	22. _____________
3. _____________	13. _____________	23. _____________
4. _____________	14. _____________	24. _____________
5. _____________	15. _____________	25. _____________
6. _____________	16. _____________	26. _____________
7. _____________	17. _____________	27. _____________
8. _____________	18. _____________	28. _____________
9. _____________	19. _____________	29. _____________
10. _____________	20. _____________	30. _____________

Make your calculations of percentages in the space below.

ACTIVITY RECORD

Name ___________________________________ Date ___________

Analyze and Conclude

Write the answers to the questions in your book on the lines below.

1. ____

____

____

2. ____

____

____

____

3. ____

____

____

____

UNIT G

Name_______________________________________ Date__________

UNIT PROJECT LINK

Make a list of healthful consumer products and services that you or people you know buy or use.

____

____

____

____

____

____

____

____

____

____

Make a list of unhealthful consumer products and services that you or people you know buy or use.

____

____

____

____

____

____

____

____

____

____

Share this information with your group.

INVESTIGATE FURTHER

Name _________________________________ Date ___________

Record the name of the genetic disorder you researched.

Describe the cause of this genetic disorder.

Describe the symptoms of this genetic disorder.

Describe any treatments for this genetic disorder.

Record the names of the sources you used for your research.

Name _______________________________________ Date __________

INVESTIGATION 1

1. What is fertilization? Describe the development of a human being from fertilization to birth.

____

____

____

____

____

____

____

2. Many scientists worldwide are currently working on the Human Genome Project, in which they are identifying the genes on each human chromosome. Explain how you think this information will be useful.

____

____

____

____

____

Each combination in the list below represents a blood type of an individual person. Remember that A and B are dominant genes, while O is a recessive gene. For each combination, tell which blood type the person has.

AA ____

AB ____

AO ____

OO ____

BO ____

Name ___________________________________ Date ___________

STAGES OF LIFE

Procedure

Make a list in the space below of the stages you think people go through as they grow and develop. For each stage, list some physical and mental characteristics you think are typical of that stage.

Analyze and Conclude

Write the answer to the question in your book on the lines below.

____

____

____

____

ACTIVITY RECORD

Name _______________________________________ Date ___________

DIFFERENT INTERESTS

Procedure

Make a list of various categories of interests you can think of. For each of these categories you will be able to write questions for your survey.

____

____

____

____

Write your predictions about whether the interests of people older than you and people younger than you are different.

____

____

____

____

Make up your survey on a separate sheet of paper. Write 20 questions. Include questions from each of the categories you listed. Then survey students and adults of different ages. Make copies of your survey for each person to complete. Keep the original blank copy in your *Science Notebook*.

Write a comparison of your survey results with the results of other groups.

____

____

____

____

Analyze and Conclude

Write the answers to the questions in your book on the lines below.

1. ____

____

ACTIVITY RECORD

CHAPTER **1**

Name ____ Date _____________

2. ____

____

____

3. ____

____

____

____

Record the names of the magazines you examined. For each, tell which age group you think the magazine is written for.

What are some of the topics you found for each group?

Children:

Teens:

Adults:

How do the illustrations and kinds of articles compare?

Name ____ Date ___________

INVESTIGATION 2

1. List and describe the major stages of human growth and development.

____

____

____

____

____

2. Many toy and game manufacturers print on the packages the ages for which their products are intended. Based on what you've learned, why is this information needed?

____

____

____

____

In the space below, make a flow chart that shows how hormones are involved in the start of puberty. At some point, your flow chart should branch into two flow charts to show differences in the process for boys and for girls.

CHAPTER WRAP-UP

Name _________________________________ Date ___________

THE HUMAN LIFE CYCLE

What is fertilization and what is the result?

____

____

____

____

How are traits passed on during reproduction?

____

____

____

____

How are a human zygote, embryo, and fetus related?

____

____

____

____

What are the stages of human growth and what are their characteristics?

____

____

____

____

____

____

What is puberty?

____

____

____

CHAPTER WRAP-UP

Use with page G27.

Name _________________________________ Date _________

Think about what you learned in Chapter 1 when you answer the following questions.

1. What surprised you most as you read "The Human Life Cycle"?

____

____

____

____

____

2. What did you think was the most interesting thing you read about human reproduction?

____

____

____

____

____

3. What did you learn about people of your own age as you read the chapter?

____

____

____

____

____

4. What else would you like to learn about the human life cycle? What could you do to find out?

____

____

____

____

____

Name _______________________________________ Date _____________

The Immune System

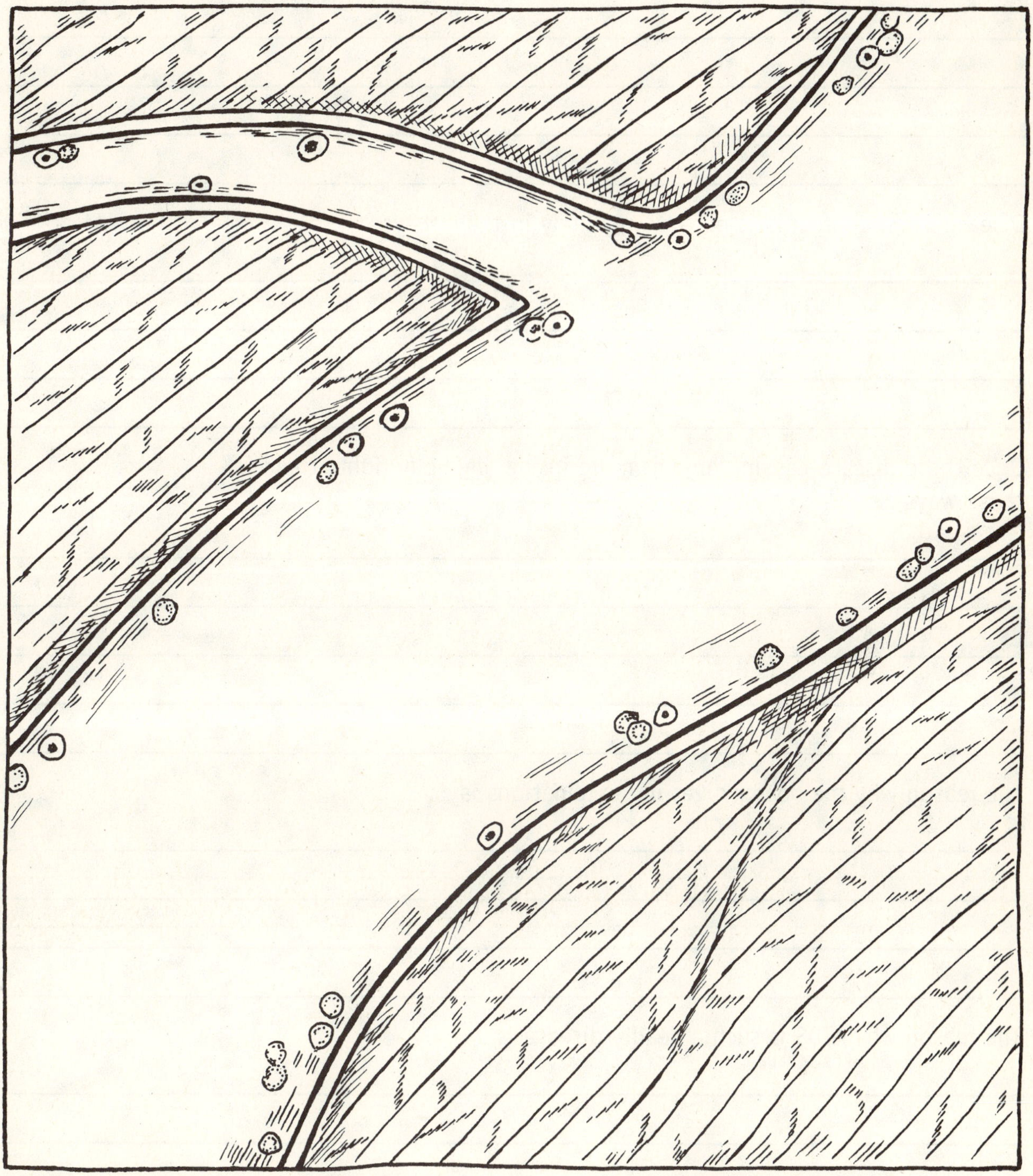

The bloodstream has been invaded by disease-causing organisms—germs!
Draw how you imagine these invaders might look. And draw some of the
body's cells fighting back.

Name _______________________________ Date ___________

Dear Journal,

I think microbes include these kinds of organisms . . .

____

____

____

____

Disease-causing organisms get into my body in these ways . . .

____

____

____

____

Once these disease-causing organism are inside, my body fights them in
these ways . . .

____

____

____

____

The reason why the doctor gives me vaccinations is . . .

____

____

____

The reason why AIDS is such a deadly disease is . . .

____

____

____

ACTIVITY RECORD

CHAPTER 2

Name _______________________________ Date ____________

MULTIPLYING MICROBES

Procedure

Write your predictions of how many bacteria there would be at the end
of five hours and at the end of ten hours.

____

____

Record your calculations of how many bacteria there would be at the
end of five hours and at the end of ten hours.

____

____

Analyze and Conclude

Write the answers to the questions in your book on the lines below.

1. ____

____

____

2. ____

____

____

____

Name _______________________________ **Date** _________

THE IMPORTANCE OF A PEEL

Procedure

Write your predictions of what will happen to the two apples over the next three days.

____

____

Record your observations of what happens to the two apples over the next three days.

After 1 day: _____________________________________

____

After 2 days: ____________________________________

____

After 3 days: ____________________________________

____

Compare your observations with those of other groups.

____

____

Analyze and Conclude

Write the answers to the questions in your book on the lines below.

1. ____

____

____

2. ____

____

3. ____

____

____

Name _________________________________ Date _________

INVESTIGATION 1

1. Describe the body's lines of defense against infection and tell how each line of defense protects the body from disease.

____

____

____

____

____

____

2. Most states require that students have vaccinations before they start school. What is the reasoning behind this practice?

____

____

____

____

In the space below, draw a cartoon strip with three scenes. Your cartoon should star Super-Macrophage, a superhero who attacks invaders. Show how Super-Macrophage defeats the enemy, and show how this superhero calls for reinforcements.

Name ______________________________ Date __________

MAKING THE ROUNDS

Procedure

Record the names of the four students with whom you traded dropperfuls of solution. Record each name immediately after trading dropperfuls of solution.

1. ______________________________

2. ______________________________

3. ______________________________

4. ______________________________

Analyze and Conclude

Write the answers to the questions in your book on the lines below.

1. ______________________________
____
____

2. ______________________________
____
____
____
____

3. ______________________________
____
____
____

INVESTIGATE FURTHER

Name _______________________________ Date ___________

Who was Typhoid Mary and what did she do?

Describe the symptoms of typhoid fever and how it can be prevented.

Describe how health agents were able to track her down.

Name____ Date___________

UNIT PROJECT LINK

Make a concept web for products in the space below. Use each of
the categories you listed in the last Unit Project Link, on page 416,
to attach to the main heading *Products*. Then attach specific examples of products to each category.

Make a concept web for services in the space below. Use each of
the categories you listed in the last Unit Project Link to attach to
the main heading *Services*. Then attach specific examples of services to each category.

In which category would you like to concentrate your research
efforts? Give a reason for your choice.

____

____

Share this information with your group.

INVESTIGATE FURTHER

CHAPTER 2

Name ___________________________ Date ___________

Make a chart in the space below to record the names of friends and family members in your survey. Talk to at least ten people. Also **record** in this chart what each person is allergic to and what their symptoms are.

Name _______________________________ **Date** _____________

INVESTIGATION 2

1. What is a pathogen? Describe some kinds of pathogens that can challenge the immune system.

____

____

____

____

2. Mary attended a conference in another city. When she returned home, she became quite ill. She learned that others attending the conference had also become ill. Make a list of ways Mary could have picked up the pathogen that caused her illness.

____

____

____

____

____

A friend who has moved to another state writes you a letter. He says that in his new state there are mosquitoes everywhere. He's heard that mosquitoes spread diseases, and now he doesn't want to go outside because he's afraid he might catch AIDS when a mosquito bites him. Write a letter back to this friend. How can you reassure him that his fear is not based on fact?

Dear

____

____

____

____

____

CHAPTER WRAP-UP

Name _______________________________________ Date ____________

THE IMMUNE SYSTEM

Describe the lines of defense that the body has to protect itself from disease.

____

____

____

____

____

____

What is the immune system and what does it include?

____

____

____

____

____

What are the different kinds of pathogens?

____

____

____

How are an allergy and AIDS alike and how are they different?

____

____

____

____

____

CHAPTER WRAP-UP

Use with page G47.

Name _________________________________ Date __________

Think about what you learned in Chapter 2 when you answer the following questions.

1. What was the most interesting thing you learned as you read "The Immune System"?

____

____

____

____

____

2. Describe something you learned about the immune response that changed your understanding of your body's reaction to disease.

____

____

____

____

____

3. What was the most useful thing you learned as you read the chapter?

____

____

____

____

____

4. How did reading the chapter change your understanding of the disease AIDS?

____

____

____

____

Name _______________________________ Date _________

MAKING HEALTHFUL CHOICES

How do like to get your exercise? Draw some students doing what you
like best to do for exercise.

Name _______________________________ Date __________

Dear Journal,

Something risky I've done that still scares me when I think about it is . . .

____

____

____

____

Smoking, drinking, and taking drugs are all risky behaviors because . . .

____

____

____

____

The healthiest thing I do is . . .

____

____

____

____

Some foods that I like but know are not healthful if I eat a lot of them are . . .

____

____

____

____

Good personal hygiene includes . . .

____

____

____

____

Name _______________________________ Date _____________

LIFESTYLE CHECK

Procedure

Write your prediction of how healthful your lifestyle is. Write your prediction in words and then predict what your score will be on the Lifestyle Assessment. A perfect score—a perfectly healthful lifestyle—would be 80.

____

____

Record your response by the numbers below to each question in the Lifestyle Assessment on page G51. Write *always, sometimes,* or *never,* depending on which you think is the most honest answer.

1. _______________ 8. _______________ 15. _______________
2. _______________ 9. _______________ 16. _______________
3. _______________ 10. ______________ 17. _______________
4. _______________ 11. ______________ 18. _______________
5. _______________ 12. ______________ 19. _______________
6. _______________ 13. ______________ 20. _______________
7. _______________ 14. ______________

Analyze and Conclude

Write the answers to the questions in your book on the lines below.

1. ____

____

____

2. ____

____

____

____

____

____

Name _________________________ Date _________

Describe a few general goals you would like to accomplish to live a more healthful lifestyle.

Make a list of specific goals that you want to accomplish within a specific time period, such as within a few weeks. These specific goals should be ways to accomplish your general goals.

Make a list on a separate sheet of paper of the risk factors you found in your home. Keep this list in your *Science Notebook*.

What are two of the risk factors you found that you think would be the most important to correct?

What could be done to correct these risk factors?

INVESTIGATION CLOSE

CHAPTER 3

Name ___________________________________ Date ___________

INVESTIGATION 1

1. What are the three main kinds of health risk factors? How much control do you have over each kind of health risk?

____

____

____

____

2. Look again at the Lifestyle Assessment on page G51. Decide which three health risk factors included are the most important to avoid. Explain the reasons for your choices.

____

____

____

____

____

For each health risk factor in the list below, write *hereditary, environmental,* or *behavioral* to classify it into one of the three groups.

Smoking tobacco ____

Using a polluted water supply ______________________________

Being female ____

Eating too much food ______________________________________

Living with someone who smokes ____________________________

Drinking alcohol ____

Not brushing your teeth ____________________________________

Being exposed to X-rays ___________________________________

Being male ____

Letting yourself get sunburned ______________________________

ACTIVITY RECORD

Name _________________________________ Date ___________

Better Habits—Better Health

Procedure

Record your inferences of how the body is harmed by smoking.

____

____

____

Record your conclusions from comparing smokers and nonsmokers for each cause of death.

____

____

____

Record your inferences of which body systems and organs are likely to be harmed by alcohol.

____

____

____

Record your conclusions from comparing alcohol users and nonusers for each cause of death.

____

____

____

Analyze and Conclude

Write the answers to the questions in your book on the lines below.

1. ____

____

____

2. ____

____

____

ACTIVITY RECORD

Name _________________________________ Date _________

3. ____

____

____

4. ____

____

____

Record what you found in your research about how many Americans currently smoke.

Describe the trends in smoking over the last ten years.

Describe which groups of Americans are currently showing increases in the number of smokers.

Record the names of the sources you used in your research.

Name _______________________________ Date _____________

FIGURING FAT

Procedure

Record the grams of fat per serving and the total Calories per serving for each food.

____

____

____

Write your predictions of which foods will have the higher percentages of fat.

____

____

Record your calculations in the space below of the percentage of fat for each food. Use the formula on page G58.

Analyze and Conclude

Write the answers to the questions in your book on the lines below.

1. ____

____

2. ____

____

____

Name____ Date__________

UNIT PROJECT LINK

Describe the kinds of information you have gathered for the
Healthful Consumer Fair.

____

____

____

____

____

In what ways could the information you've gathered be presented
in a pamphlet or booklet so that it would be helpful for others?

____

____

____

____

____

How do you think this pamphlet or booklet should be organized?

____

____

____

____

____

What could you do in helping to prepare this pamphlet or booklet?

____

____

____

____

____

Share this information with your group.

Name _______________________________________ Date __________

INVESTIGATION 2

1. What are some good health habits that can reduce behavioral risk factors?

____

____

____

____

2. Even though it's foolish to take some kinds of risks, you can't go through life without encountering risks. Describe how you can decide which risks are worth taking and which aren't.

____

____

Study the Food Pyramid on page G59. Using what you've learned, write a menu for next Saturday's breakfast, lunch, and dinner. Make sure you include the right proportions of the different types of foods.

Name _________________________________ Date _________

MAKING HEALTHFUL CHOICES

What is a health risk factor and how are health risk factors classified?

____

____

____

____

____

What are five behavioral risk factors that a person has some control over?

____

____

____

____

____

____

____

____

____

What foods should form the base of a healthful diet?

____

____

____

What are the benefits of regular exercise?

____

____

____

____

CHAPTER WRAP-UP

Name _______________________________________ Date ___________

Think about what you learned in Chapter 3 when you answer the following questions.

1. What did you learn in reading "Making Healthful Choices" that you think could be beneficial to your life?

____

____

____

____

____

2. What did you learn in reading the chapter that might make you think twice about engaging in risky behavior?

____

____

____

____

____

3. What did you learn about smoking tobacco and drinking alcohol that might convince someone close to you to quit smoking or abusing alcohol?

____

____

____

____

____

4. Among all the behavioral health risk factors, which would you most like to eliminate in your life?

____

____

____

____

UNIT G

Name_______________________________ Date__________

UNIT PROJECT WRAP-UP

Think about the Unit Project Big Event you helped plan and present—the Healthful Consumer Fair. Which pamphlet, prop, audiovisual aid, or presentation did you think was most effective in explaining why a healthful lifestyle is something to be desired?

____

____

____

____

Which part of the fair did you think best put across the idea that people can make themselves healthy by changing their habits?

____

____

____

____

Which part of the fair do you think presented information that those who attended did not previously know?

____

____

____

____

Tell what you were most proud to have helped prepare for the Healthful Consumer Fair.

____

____

____